The Mining Boom of 2004

Martin Lynch

ISBN: 978-1-922460-99-8 (paperback)

Published in Australia by Martin Lynch and InHouse Publishing.
www.inhousepublishing.com.au

Printed in Australia by InHouse Print & Design.

IN HOUSE PTY LTD PUBLISHING

NATIONAL LIBRARY OF AUSTRALIA

A catalogue record for this book is available from the National Library of Australia

Contents

Introduction v

Chapter 1: THE BUILD-UP

The Agricultural Revolution 1

Chinese Mining in the 1980s 4

China Becomes a Force in Global Manufacturing 7

Global Mining at the End of the 1990s 10

Chapter 2: TEN HECTIC YEARS

The Housing Boom 19

The Price Hikes 24

The Chinese Response 27

Chapter 3: THE IMPACT ON GLOBAL MINING

Mined Copper 34

Bauxite 39

Coal 44

Iron Ore 49

Chapter 4: THE AFTERMATH

The Party Comes to an End 57

When the Dust Settled 60

Six Years On 64

References 71

Introduction

This book deals with the global mining boom of 2004. It looks at its origins, how it unfolded and its aftermath. It is the second in a series of four books which deal with how global industrialisation shapes and drives the global mining industry.

It is necessary to be clear about what a mining boom actually is. Essentially, a mining boom occurs when the benchmark prices of a broad range of minerals rise sharply and for a sustained period, typically several years or more. This is what happened in global mineral markets beginning in 2004.

Prices, as any economist will tell you, are determined by the interaction of supply and demand. The demand side of the mining boom was all about China, its post-Mao economic reforms and the rapid industrialisation and urbanisation which those reforms drove. Indeed, if the boom of 2004 can be said have had a single cause, then it was the decision of the Chinese government to sell-off its huge stock of urban housing. That action created very active housing markets in China's cities where there had been practically none before. A massive and sustained bout of high-rise apartment construction followed.

The supply side contributed to the situation too. This happened mainly because, when China's demand for minerals shot upwards in the wake of the privatisation of government-owned housing, the country had to turn to foreign miners because its own domestic miners could not cope. When the Chinese came knocking, the miners in the wider world were unprepared. They were in a defensive, cost-cutting mode, not geared up for expansion. After all, business conditions had been so poor for so long that benchmark prices for most minerals and metals were at record lows. Which helps explain why the price rises over the next few years were so sharp and so large.

Mining booms of the 2004 variety are rare events. Indeed, the mineral price rises which happened in its first three years had almost no precedent in history, the only comparable rises were those seen during the early years of the First World War. Because of this, the whole episode merits a closer look in order to draw out the industry dynamics which underpinned it. Hence this book.

The book is in four chapters. The first deals with the lead-up to the mining boom, discussing how China embarked on, and then continued, its rapid industrialisation through the 1980s and 90s. Also discussed is how Chinese and foreign miners were performing through the 1990s: their fortunes during those ten years were quite different.

Chapters 2 and 3 look at the mining boom itself. In Chapter 2, the drivers of China's huge mineral demand are discussed, as are the subsequent price hikes and the Chinese domestic response. In Chapter 3, the four largest mining sectors are examined to look at the different global supply-side responses to China's demand. The four sectors are copper, bauxite, iron ore and coal. There are of course many other sectors which could have been looked at but to include more sectors would make the book overly long, and probably fairly tedious, without shedding much additional light on the subject.

Chapter 4 looks at the end of the boom: what brought it to an end and how it changed the face of global mining. The biggest change is that nowadays most of the world's smelting capacity is located in China, where prior to the year 2000 it was widely distributed across many countries. Never in history has such a concentration been seen. It is likely to be an enduring change and one which will have big influence on the global mining industry for decades to come.

Chapter 1

THE BUILD-UP

The Agricultural Revolution

In one way of looking at it, the road to the mining boom of 2004 began with the death of Chairman Mao, Communist China's first paramount leader. When Mao died in 1976, the China he left behind was amongst the poorest countries in the world. Hunger was an ever-present reality for many. So too were crowded and unsanitary living conditions. The average floorspace per person in the cities was about five square metres. Most families shared cooking, toilet and washing facilities with a group of other families. In about one third of apartments, two families lived together in a single room. This was hardly different from the early 1950s when China was just emerging from its 100 hundred years of foreign occupation and civil war. In other words, thirty years of Communist rule had brought the common people little more than slogans. So it was that in 1976, with Chairman Mao secure in his mausoleum, his successors were faced with an unhappy populace impatient for change.

China's post-Mao leadership all agreed that the country had to get on the path of economic progress. There was disagreement, however, about which path to get onto. One option was to keep going with Mao's emphasis on heavy industry and continue building power plants, steel mills and cement factories. The other option was to switch the emphasis to light industry and start building more houses and apartment blocks and producing more clothes and footwear. The heavy industry camp was led by Mao's anointed successor, Hua Guofeng. He proposed the construction of ten new steel mills to be built over ten years, including a giant integrated works in Shanghai, and another in Wuhan. The light industry camp was led by Deng Xiaoping. His priority was the feeding, clothing and housing of the people. Steel was not even on his list. Deng won the struggle for power and by the time of the Party conference in December 1978 he was the undisputed leader of China.

Just as the first era of Communist leadership was dominated by Mao Zedong, the second era came to be dominated by Deng Xiaoping. He had long clashed with Chairman Mao. One (slightly exaggerated) way to describe their differences is to say that Mao favoured economic policies which were in keeping with Communist doctrine, regardless of whether they were effective, whereas Deng favoured economic policies which were effective, regardless of whether they were in keeping with Communist doctrine. Deng had expressed this attitude as far back as 1961: "It doesn't matter whether the cat is black or yellow. As long as it catches mice it is a good cat."[1] (In the modern version of that quote, the non-black cat is white.) So with Deng now in power, China was about to enter a very different economic era.

The first and most pressing task was to increase the harvest. In the Mao era, China's farming regions had been transformed into the Maoist version of farming factories. These factories, or Agricultural Communes as they were called, consisted of the combined land of five or six thousand peasant families. The peasants deeply resented the loss of independence and they responded by putting in a half-hearted effort out in the fields. The result was that harvests never came up to where they should be. The Party leadership knew that the quickest way to turn the situation around was to give the farms back to the farmers. So it was that between 1979 and 1982 rural China shifted from being organized into about 50,000 Agricultural Communes to being fragmented into over one hundred million household-run farms. It was a nation-wide agricultural revolution.

The impact on the harvest was immediate. Between 1981 and 1984, national grain production increased by 82 million tonnes, and grain production per person went from 325kg to 393kg. In just those three years, the Chinese rural areas went from being dour and lifeless to vibrant and entrepreneurial.[2]

The markets in the country towns came alive as farmers gathered to sell the produce of their small market gardens, and to spend the money which they were earning from their grain sales. Shortages of all sorts of consumer items – clothing, footwear, bicycles, furniture and so on – quickly developed. Items of farming equipment such as water pumps and two-wheeled tractors were also in demand, and soon were also hard to get.

The shortages spelled opportunity for the local towns and a thriving rural light manufacturing sector came into being. These town-based factories pulled millions of farm workers off the farms. The available spare housing was soon taken, so construction on residential accommodation began the length and breadth of China. Soon it had become one of China's major industries. To quantify the scale of the effort: in 1980 there were about 180 million people living in the villages, towns and cities of China each on average occupying a residential floorspace of about six square metres. Over the next ten years a further 100 million people moved in, for each of these an average floorspace of ten square metres was built. Through the course of the 1980s, the total stock of urban residential floorspace rose from about one billion square metres to two billion. Town-based manufacturing and construction became the engine of Chinese economic growth through the 1980s.

It was a development that took everyone by surprise. As Deng Xiaoping said in 1987: "In the rural reform, our greatest success – and it is one we had by no means anticipated – has been the emergence of a large number of enterprises run by villages and towns. They were like a new force that just came into being spontaneously."

Chinese Mining in the 1980s

The unexpected success of the agricultural reforms launched China into a new era of industrialisation and urbanisation. It needed metals, energy and other materials as never before. Because of the country's aging production base, built mostly in the 1950s, there was never enough of anything.

It should be made clear that China, even as the reform era was beginning, was already home to a mining and smelting industry of global importance. Its largest sector was coal, where China was the third-highest producer in the world. China also ranked third in cement production. In steel, only four countries produced more than China, and they were the world's largest industrial nations: the United States, the Soviet Union, Japan and Germany. China was also fifth in iron ore production. For good measure, it also ranked fifth in the world in lead and sixth in tin mine output.[3]

In other base metals, the country was not so active, nor well-endowed. In copper, aluminium, zinc and nickel production, it did not make the top 10. Still, there were other sectors where it was the largest producer in the world. These included tungsten, fluorspar, antimony, molybdenum and talc.

Large as it was, the country's mining and smelting production base could not keep up with the demands which were placed upon it as the nation's farming regions sprang back to life. This is because it was aging and running out of in-built expansion capacity. Much of it had been built with the help of Soviet engineers back in the 1950s. Now it was in need of major expansion. It was holding the country back.

The aging production base was not alone in holding the country back. The congested railway system was doing the same thing. Put simply, China's rail transport network was a fundamental part of the mining-smelting value chain and it was nowhere near adequate for a country as vast and populous as China. To provide a comparison: the USA and China are about the same size in terms of land area. In 1880, the USA with a population of 50 million people, had a rail network which was 58,000 kilometres in total length. In 1980, China with a population of nearly one billion people, had a network of 53,000 kilometres. As a result, the railway system was constantly and severely overloaded. Railway construction never got anything like the investment it needed.

It was common knowledge that something had to be done about the railway network, but it was too large and complex to be quickly sorted out. So the focus turned to how to expand the country's mining and smelting base without relying too heavily on the railway system. It is because the Baosteel project presented a solution to that issue that it can be considered to be the opening act in the transformation of the metallurgical industries of China.

The Baosteel project needs an introduction.[4] Essentially it was a large coastal steel mill designed to be fed with imported iron ore and coal. By shipping the iron ore and coal in from overseas, no extra load was placed on China's rail system. Such a project would have been unthinkable during the Mao years. But the Mao years died along with Mao. After his death, it did not take long for new ideas to emerge. Or rather, it did not take long for the Chinese to start borrowing ideas from overseas. Which is why, in 1977, just six months after Mao's state funeral, talks began with Nippon Steel to build a Japanese-style world-class steel mill somewhere on the coast of China. The location chosen for this revolutionary new mill was a desolate marsh area on the shore of the Yangtze River, some twenty kilometres from downtown Shanghai. It was in a district called Baoshan, and so the project came to be known as Baosteel.

The Baosteel project was actually intended to provide solutions to two problems. One was China's overloaded railway system. The other was the poor quality of Chinese iron ore. As early as the 1920s, geologists knew two things about China's iron ore resources: there were vast quantities of it, and most of it was very low grade.[5] Starting during the 1950s, there had been a continual nationwide search for new deposits. Plenty had been found, but the sought-after high grade ores had not been. The Chinese government had reluctantly concluded that the future of its iron ore supplies depended, in large part, on foreign mines. So it was that construction at Baoshan began in 1978 and the first pig iron was poured in September 1984. It was a welcome development, because by then China was in the middle of its rural construction boom.

The Baoshan development was one of many. Through the 1980s, the pressure on the country's mines and smelters was relentless. The Party leadership placed priority on the production of four materials: coal, steel, cement and aluminium. Over the course of the 1980s, production from Chinese steel mills nearly doubled[6] and in aluminium it nearly tripled. There was a new aluminium smelter commissioned every year. Fushun, by far the biggest smelter in the country in 1980, had been joined by four others of equal size by 1990. In coal, production increased from a little over 600 million to well over one billion tonnes.

All of this activity, and much more besides, had made China one of the leading mining nations in the world by 1990.[7] It was the largest coal producer, the largest cement producer, number two in iron ore, tenth in mined copper and also tenth in bauxite. As for metal production, it was fourth in steel, fifth in copper and sixth in aluminium.

With domestic demand growing so fast, it might be expected that China would have resorted to importing more and more coal and metals. But the country's mining and smelting sectors managed to keep pace with demand. Chinese engineers developed a real skill in building projects quickly and cheaply.[8] These facilities were not exactly leading edge when it came to safety and waste management, but hazard and pollution was something the Party leadership was prepared to live with as it pushed for more production and construction.

Even so, it was clear that in the long-term the country's rate of mine development could not be sustained.[9] For this reason, smelters began to adopt the Japanese practice of entering long-term contracts for purchasing foreign ores. The first important one had been finalised in 1987. It was a joint venture between Baosteel and the Australian iron ore producer, Hamersley Iron. The Channar Joint Venture, as it was called, provided for the shipment to Baosteel of ten million tonnes per year of high grade iron ore. The first shipment arrived at Baoshan in early 1990.

China Becomes a Force in Global Manufacturing

If it was the agricultural reforms which drove the Chinese economy in the 1980s, it was the growth of the export sector which drove it in the 1990s. Over that decade, China went from being a small player in global trade to one of the leading trading nations of the world.

The reform which drove this was actually enacted in the late 1970s. Like many important reforms, it took some time to bear fruit. The reform in question was the establishment of the Special Economic Zones, or SEZs. In 1979, in an effort to draw modern manufacturing techniques into China from the outside world, the Chinese government had established four of these SEZs. The intention was to attract foreign companies to set-up inside China, employing Chinese workers who would then become skilled in the latest techniques. The four were located in coastal towns near to Hong Kong and Taiwan. The hope was that businesses from those two prosperous Chinese-speaking countries would make the move to the mainland.

Through the 1980s it was slow-going in three of the four, but one of them did take-off. That was Shenzhen, which in 1980 was an impoverished city of 50,000 people, most of whom earned their living from fishing or farming. The great advantage which Shenzhen had was that it was located right on China's land border with Hong Kong, and lay only thirty kilometres from the city centre. It was therefore worthwhile for Chinese-speaking Hong Kong manufacturers to move their factories to take advantage of the low wages and cheap land on offer in Shenzhen – as long as they could access all the communications, electrical power, running water and transport facilities that they had in Hong Kong. The Chinese government poured in money, then more money, to build the necessary infrastructure, and by the end of the 1980s Shenzhen had become a flourishing manufacturing city of one million people, generating 1% of China's national GDP. The other SEZs, which by 1989 were seven in number, were nowhere near as successful.

From this distance in time, it may appear that China's reform era was one uninterrupted success story, but this is not the case. By the end of the 1980s serious tensions were growing within the Chinese leadership. The upheaval caused by the agricultural reforms, and the outright failure of attempts to reform the city-based factories, had taken their toll. In the view of some of China's top leaders, the reforms were going too fast and sections of the population were becoming too bold, demanding ever more freedoms. Their fears were confirmed when, following the state funeral of the popular Hu Yaobang, a massive crowd of students gathered in Beijing's Tienanmen Square to honour him. The crowd stayed on after the funeral, and their mourning turned to protest. For many in the Communist Party leadership – even in the reformer faction – the protests were an intolerable provocation. Anger grew on both sides until, on June 4, 1989, the military were sent in to clear the Square. In the process they killed between 200 (the official death toll) and 10,000 (estimates of foreign observers) people. The event shocked China, and brought the economy to a sudden halt.

So it was that, as 1990 dawned, growth in the Chinese economy had stalled, and there was a tense stand-off between the two main factions of the Chinese leadership: the conservatives and the reformers. If the conservatives had prevailed, the mining boom probably would never have happened, and certainly would not have begun in 2004. As it turned out, the reformers carried the day, largely thanks to the political skills of Deng Xiaoping.

Once the reformers were back in the driving seat, the 1990s turned into another decade of record-breaking economic growth.

Everything seemed to go right. The Special Economic Zones roared into life, propelled along by a new wave of business migration from Hong Kong, a massive shift of Taiwan's factory system to mainland China and a steadily increasing inflow of manufacturers from the United States and Europe. Not to be out-done, domestic Chinese companies, especially those which were privately-owned, began to manufacture for export as well as for domestic consumption.

By the end of the decade China was the world's largest manufacturing-for-export nation. Where once the label Made in Hong Kong was a fixture on toys, plastic goods and simple electric appliances, now it was Made in China. The country also produced a big share of the world's white goods and more complex electrical items such as TVs and mobile phones. To give some statistics: in 2001, China manufactured one quarter of the world's washing machines, one third of its air conditioners, microwaves and colour TVs, half of its cameras and phones, and more than two thirds of its DVD players.

The Pearl River Delta, home to Shenzhen and a host of other cities, was the biggest centre of China's export factories. Shanghai and its hinterland was not far behind. In both regions, by the late 1990s, industrial parks stretched for miles in every direction. The horizon was punctuated by power stations pluming their smoke into the sky.

All of this manufacturing activity needed workers. The workforce in the cities was already taken, so they flocked in from the farms. So many of them came that a population explosion took in place in the coastal cities. The Pearl River Delta saw the largest increase. Its population grew from seven to twenty six million over the decade. Shenzhen was the stand-out: it went from being home to one million people in 1990 to being home to more than six million ten years later. As for Shanghai, China's largest city, it was home to nearly eight million people in 1990 and that had risen to over fourteen million by the end of the decade. It all created a big demand for new residential accommodation. China's coastal cities turned into construction sites, none more so than Shanghai. Its Pudong district was forest of cranes.

Global Mining at the End of the 1990s

With all of this factory and residential accommodation construction, the expansion of China's domestic mining and smelting base continued through the 1990s. Steelworks, cement kilns, aluminium and copper smelters and coal-fired power stations were needed in always greater quantities. Such was the growth that in 1996 China had become the leading steel producer in the world, and its iron ore production easily exceeded that of any other country. By that time it was also by far the largest producer of coal and cement, as well as being third in the world in production of aluminium and fifth in bauxite. It was ranked fourth in refined copper, and had even climbed to seventh in the production of mined copper. With all of this going on, the domestic mines were definitely feeling the strain, and China was turning to foreign supplies of finished metal. One third of its domestic requirements of copper were imported, and roughly the same percentage of aluminium.

Given this colossus-in-the-making just two hundred kilometres from Japan, it might be assumed that China's smelting industries would have moved into the centre of attention of the miners in the outside world. But they had not. China remained on the periphery. The focus of the big miners continued to be on the smelters in Japan, North America and Western Europe.

Times were tough in those markets. In every sector – coal, steel, aluminium, copper, nickel, zinc and so on – prices had been on a declining trend for twenty five years. By the late 1990s, in real terms, global benchmark prices were less than half what they had been in the early 1970s. In some cases, they were lower than they had been during the Great Depression.[10]

At first glance it seemed obvious what the cause was: excluding China, the global demand for coal and metals had been stalled for decades. Or, to put it in a more long-winded way, the post-war boom era of urbanisation and manufacturing in the western countries had ended in the 1970s, with the result that consumption of energy and metals in those countries had slowed dramatically in the 1980s, and had ground to a halt in the 1990s.

Exhibit A in support of this was the global consumption of finished steel outside of China. It had hardly moved over the course of the 1990s. Exhibit B was the global consumption of coal outside of China. It had actually fallen by 10% over the decade. Exhibit C was the global consumption of aluminium outside of China. Over the 1990s it had grown at just 1.1% per year, a glacial rate of increase compared to the 1960s and 70s.

First glances can sometimes be deceiving, and in this case a second glance reveals a different picture. On closer inspection, the cause of the stalled global demand was not a general western world slowdown. It was actually a screeching halt in one major country. As it turns out, the main cause of the stagnant state of global mining during the 1990s was the collapse of the economy of the Soviet Union. When it collapsed it took with it a lot of the world's demand for coal and metals. Steel consumption in the former Soviet Republics plunged from 116 million tonnes in 1990 to 26 million tonnes in 1994, and had further slumped to 20 million by 1999.[1] It was a similar story for coal, aluminium, copper and cement. Having been the world's second or third highest consumer of most metals and coal, the former Soviet Union was, by the mid 1990s, a minor player on the world stage.

It was the collapse of the Soviet Union which caused the stagnation of global (outside China) coal and metal consumption during 1990s. But the Soviet Union's economy was fairly isolated from the rest of the world. Which meant that the collapse of the Soviet Union was an event which did not really spill out into the wider world of mining and metals. Which raises the question: if the collapse of the Soviet Union did not impact global metal markets very much, why had benchmark prices around the world fallen so low by the end of the 1990s? There is no single answer to this. Each sector had its own dynamic. Common to them all however was the fact that the 1990s were a time of falling production costs in mining.

Mine production costs had been on a downward trend since the 1970s. The largest contributor had been the weakening of trade union power. That had resulted in lower labour costs and, more importantly, greatly increased labour and machinery productivity. This trend had been reinforced by the adoption of ever-larger machinery in both the mine and the processing plants. As production costs fell, they allowed the mining of lower grade ores, thereby raising production without any major new investment.

The result was a tendency to oversupply in every major mining sector, which in turn created further downward pressure on prices. In addition to these general forces driving down prices, the four sectors of coal, iron ore, copper and aluminium all had their own particular dynamic which was driving prices down. These sector-specific dynamics will now be discussed.

Coal

In coal, the sector-specific factor which drove prices to historic lows was the closure of the European coal mines. To explain why closing the coal mines drove the price down (and not up) some history is needed. In the 1970s Europe's coal mines were the highest cost producers in the world. They were geologically complex and difficult to mine, so they had an in-built high cost of mining. Adding to this was the fact that they were operated by an expensive and not very efficient workforce whose wages and working conditions were protected by militant trade unions. The governments of Europe tended to tiptoe around the coal regions. The mines were seen as vital sources of employment, and the politicians did not want to face the political backlash which would accompany any intervention.

That began to change in the 1980s. A new breed of politicians came to power wanting to unleash a new wave of productivity in their moribund economies. The leaders of the movement were Ronald Reagan in the United States and Margaret Thatcher in the United Kingdom. Thatcher engaged in an epic battle with the British coal miners, eventually winning the fight. The workforce at British

Coal was some 250,000 in 1980 and it had fallen to 10,000 by the mid 1990s.[11] Coal production had fallen from 150 million tonnes to 30 million. Similar outcomes were achieved, although with a lot less conflict, elsewhere in Europe.

It might be expected that such a drastic fall in output would drive coal prices much higher. But the opposite happened. European coal mines it turned out did not have a stranglehold on the continent's energy supply. Two alternative sources of energy filled the gap left by the shuttered mines. One was Russian natural gas, which started to flow in great quantities in the late 1980s, taking much of the market for coal. The other was coal from Australia, South Africa and the United States, which was far cheaper than the local variety. The result was that coal prices in Europe fell steeply through the decade, and this spread to every other coal market. By 1998, the benchmark price for thermal coal had hit its lowest level in a century.

Iron ore

In iron ore, the sector-specific cause of the historic low prices which had been reached in the 1990s was a very different one. The low prices could be attributed to the sublime negotiating skills of the Japanese steel cartel.

As in coal, the collapse of the Soviet Union had not affected the wider global iron ore sector. This is because the iron ores of Russia and Ukraine were low grade and had to be pelletised before use. This made them expensive. When the transport costs to get them to international markets were thrown in, Russian and Ukrainian pellets were very expensive on the international market. So the Soviet iron ore, instead of going onto the export market, stayed in the ground.

The Soviet Union was not the only region with an iron ore market isolated from the rest of the world. This sort of market also existed in North America, India and China. In each case there was a domestic iron ore mining sector, supplemented by some imports, which supplied a domestic steel industry. There were only two steel-making regions of any size which operated in a global market for iron ore. They were

Western Europe and the East Asian countries of Japan, Taiwan and South Korea. Both were dependent on imported iron ore which was delivered to them in big ocean-going bulk carriers. This iron ore came mostly from Brazil and Australia. It was in this "seaborne" market that the global benchmark price for iron ore was determined.[12]

Supply to the seaborne market was dominated by the Big Three producers – CVRD in Brazil, and Rio Tinto and BHP in Australia. They held the lion's share of production capacity in the late 1990s. Australia's Robe River and a few others formed a second tier. It was a consolidated industry which had long practiced supply-side discipline. That meant that any major capacity expansions – especially of the port and railway – were few and far between, and were telegraphed far in advance.

Given this careful approach to capacity addition on the part of the iron ore producers, it might be expected that the price of iron ore would be continually pushed up, or at least stay steady. After all, the steel makers of Western Europe and East Asia were captive customers. They had nowhere else to go for their iron ore. They should have been, to use an economic term, "price takers". So why was it that in 1998 the price for seaborne iron ore was at record lows? It was one third of the level of 1978. That was an even steeper fall than in the over-supplied sectors of copper and aluminium. How did it happen?

In short, the highly-disciplined iron ore producers were always outplayed by their better-prepared customers, the Japanese and European steel cartels. The cartels each year hosted stage-managed price negotiations which pitted the iron ore producers against each other. This allowed the cartels to keep pushing prices down when, if market forces had been allowed to prevail, the price would have gone up. Perhaps the reason this could happen lies in the cost structure of the miners. Even with prices at the historic lows they reached in the early 2000s, they were still comfortably profitable. It should be noted that when the China mining boom finally liberated them from the dominance of the Japanese, the Big Three became a lot more than comfortably profitable. They became cash generating machines.

Copper

In copper, the sector-specific cause of the historically low prices of the late 1990s and early 2000s was a great surge of new production capacity added between 1990 and 2000. It far exceeded the world's ability to absorb it.

Three quarters of this new capacity was constructed in Chile. To put some numbers around it: Chile, already ranked number 1 in the world in copper production, lifted its mined copper output from 1.6 million tonnes in 1990 to 4.5 million tonnes in 2000. A dozen major mines came into production during those ten years including Escondida in 1990, Cerro Colorado in 1994, Candelaria, Zaldivar and Radomiro Tomic in 1995 and El Abra in 1996. Then at the end of the decade, a major expansion of Escondida came on-stream as well as two new mines of global significance, Collahuasi and Los Pelambres.[13]

Supporting this great expansion, there was a threefold increase in capacity over the course of the 1990s at the Indonesian mine of Grasberg. That added another 0.7 million tonnes per year by 2000. Then there was the additional 0.5 million tonnes per year which spilled out into the international markets after the collapse of the Soviet Union. All up, global copper supply increased by about 4.5% per year over the 1990s. In the previous two decades it had grown at about 1.5%. It was this surge of new production which had driven the price of copper down to Depression-era levels by the early 2000s.

The trigger for this procession of new Andean mine developments was the return to democracy in Chile. Here some history is needed. During the 1970s and 1980s, General Pinochet's brutal dictatorship ruled over Chile, and a government-owned copper monopoly, Codelco, ruled over Chilean copper mining. The copper mines had been fully nationalised in 1973 by the left-wing Salvador Allende. When Pinochet seized power from Allende, foreigners expected him to reverse the nationalisation but he had kept it in place and even went a step further: he created Codelco to better administer it. Inside Chile, this was a popular policy.[14]

This Chile-only policy was relaxed in 1980 when it was realised that just how expensive and difficult copper mine developments could be. Foreign companies were once more permitted to invest in Chilean mining. That move did not have much impact because foreign bankers and investors did not trust the Pinochet government, just as they did not trust South American governments more generally. The result was that no foreign-funded mine development happened in the 1980s. But there was plenty of foreign investment in mineral exploration. Throughout the 1980s aerial surveys, deep drilling and other geological work was carried on. An inventory of major orebody discoveries accumulated. These orebodies were of all shapes and sizes: some were very large and some were not, some were close to the surface and some were quite deep, some were high grade and others not, and some were free of nasty chemicals like arsenic, while others contained high levels of them.

The mood inside Chile was changing in the late 1980s. Pinochet decided to follow the constitution he had written and so he held a "return to democracy" plebiscite in 1988.[15] Soon after, democratic elections were held which resulted in a civilian government for the first time in 15 years. In foreign banking head offices this was taken as a signal that Chile's great copper orebodies were now open for business. It was like a starter's gun had been fired. Every major mining company in the world joined the race to open a brand new Andean copper mine. Everyone wanted the good ones before somebody else got them.

The result was a wave of new mine development such that, by the year 2000, Chilean copper production had tripled from its level in 1990. There was an inevitable cost to doing that. As production went up, prices went down. By the end of the decade the benchmark copper price had fallen to the point where it had been lower in only one other year – 1931, the darkest year of the Great Depression. It did not stop there. Production kept climbing and prices falling. In 2003 the inflation-adjusted copper price hit its lowest ever level since reliable data-keeping began in the 1860s.

Aluminium

Even in aluminium, prices reached near-record lows in 1999. Then they fell to all-time lows three years later. There was no particular sector-specific driver of this. The cause was a general one. It was what might be called, to contrast it with the situation in iron ore, supply-side indiscipline. It had simply become too easy to build aluminium smelters. Adding to the problem was the fact that there was a ready supply of bauxite to feed the new smelters, thanks to big resource discoveries made in the 1960s and 70s in Australia.[16] The result of that over-expansion was a long-term downward trend in aluminium prices. The low point was reached in 2002, just before the mining boom began. In that year, the benchmark price was less than half what it had been in the 1950s.

So it was that the global mining industry on the eve of the mining boom was in the doldrums. Record low prices all around, and no obvious prospect of improvement. That was about to change.

Chapter 2

TEN HECTIC YEARS

The Housing Boom

Although the Chinese economy was growing a great rate in the first half of the 1990s, the policymakers in Beijing knew that it would not last unless they faced the "elephant in the room". The elephant was the chronically underperforming state-owned businesses. Their performance was hardly better than it had been during the Mao years despite the fact that China was changing and modernising in every other area.

The task of reforming them fell to Zhu Rong-Ji. There was no better choice than Zhu. He had been Party boss of Shanghai and in that position had been the driving force behind the massive Pudong development. Then he had been responsible for the successful restructuring of China's taxation system, which resulted in bringing the nation's Treasury back into the black. The job of reforming the country's state-owned businesses was his toughest assignment so far. It had already defeated reformers of the calibre of Deng Xiaoping and Zhao Ziyang.

The trouble was that the state-owned businesses were not really businesses at all. They were welfare agencies which derived their income from producing some goods or services. They took on the responsibility for providing everything that their workers and their workers' families needed, including education, health care, housing and retirement needs. They even provided shopping outlets. A job in one of these state-owned companies was a job for life. It was known as the "iron rice bowl" because the state guaranteed that the worker's supply of food, signified by the rice bowl, could not be broken.[17] They were not very dynamic organisations.

In the mid-1990s, despite the expansion of private industry and the now-crowded Special Economic Zones full of foreign-owned companies, it was still the case that well over half of China's city-based workers had a job in one of these state-owned enterprises. That meant that over 300 million Chinese (including children and retirees) were dependent on them. Which was why the leadership in Beijing was treading carefully.

It took a year or more of discussion before Zhu came up with a reform plan that seemed like it might work. It was approved at the 15th Communist Party Congress which was held in Beijing in September 1997. Despite the need to tread carefully, it was a radical plan. The main points:

- The larger state-owned enterprises would remain in government hands, and the smaller ones would be either privatized, handed over to local governments, or shut down altogether.
- Guaranteed employment was ended, even in the companies being kept in government ownership.
- All of the state-owned enterprises, both large and small, were to relinquish their welfare obligations. No longer would they have to provide schooling, health care and retirement benefits. Neither would they have to provide housing for their employees.
- The company housing was to be sold off. Each apartment would first be offered to the occupant, and if that offer was not taken up, it would be sold on the open market. The sale of housing was to be done at very low prices, and where the occupants did not have the savings to afford a cash payment, a low-interest loan was available.

The policy was clear: state-owned businesses large and small were now going to be run as businesses, not as Mao-era social welfare projects.

Even the best laid plans can have unintended consequences, and so it was with this reform. Its biggest impact was entirely unanticipated. At the core of that was the privatisation of government housing. In just three years between 1999 and 2001, all of China's urban housing stock fell into the hands of private owners. Many workers bought their apartment when it was offered. The purchase was probably not made with any great joy, after all Chinese families were tired of living in this cramped accommodation where they had to queue for the toilet and the kitchen. But the purchase price they had to pay was so low that it was an offer which could not be refused.

Once in possession of their apartment, the new owners started to think about upgrading. Most of them had money. They had been saving for years, as was the Chinese habit, and their wages were rising along with the powerhouse urban economy. Adding to that, they discovered that the rental income they could get from their apartment was rising all the time as more workers came into the cities needing accommodation. All of which meant that, if they wanted to upgrade, they could afford the down payment on a new apartment and the repayments on the loan. It did not take a financial genius to realise that there was a lot of pent-up demand for new city apartments. Once this realisation sank in, so began the great China housing boom.[18]

From about 2003, the construction of high-rise apartment blocks consumed the cities. It would have happened anyway given the poor state of the housing stock. But plenty of fuel was added to the fire because the migrant workers just kept on coming. The result was an apartment construction boom on an epic scale. In total, in the decade after 2000 the built-up area occupied by China's cities went from about 17,000 square kilometres to nearly 30,000. At the end of the decade, there was more than twice as much floorspace in China's cities as there had been at the beginning.

At the same time as the housing boom was transforming China's city skylines, the country's manufacturing base was growing at high speed. In the decade from 2000 to 2010, China rose from being a manufacturer of global importance to being the largest manufacturing nation on earth. Partly this was driven by the rising wealth of the average Chinese family. In short, as each year passed, the average family could afford to buy more. And in the case of those with newly-purchased apartments, they had to buy everything new to furnish their new living spaces. After all, the tattered sofas and faded curtains from their old government-owned apartment would never be good enough.

In addition to this domestic demand, four developments in the wider world of global trade had come together at the end of the 1990s and created a huge opportunity for any exporting country in the right position to benefit from them. China was in that right position and became the beneficiary of an extraordinary surge in demand for its exports of manufactured goods. The four developments were:

- *A change in the international rules of trade.* The longstanding General Agreement on Tariffs and Trade, or GATT, had been replaced by the World Trade Organisation, or WTO. This is because the GATT dealt only in tangible goods, and the economies of the western democracies were increasingly dominated by trade in intangible services. The WTO was designed to govern trade in all products: tangible goods, intangible services and intellectual property. Armed with this better framework, many of the western nations, especially the USA, were now prepared to open their borders to low cost manufactured goods from foreign countries. It was done on the understanding that their banking, telecom, education and other service sectors would be allowed unimpeded access into those same foreign countries. It was a deal which, as it turned out, was far more beneficial to the low cost manufacturing countries than it was to the high tech services-providing countries.
- *The weakening of China's competitor exporters.* In 1997 the Asian Crisis struck the industrialising South East Asian nations of Thailand, Indonesia and Malaysia. This was a fortunate

catastrophe for China because, just as it was preparing its own domestic companies to compete for export sales, three of its most formidable competitors were greatly diminished in their ability to compete.

- *The rapid expansion of the computer market.* Starting in the late 1990s the computer went from being a help in the office and at home to being a social phenomenon. Everyone from primary schoolers to their grandparents now needed all sorts of communication devices which a few years before they could not even have imagined. It drove a very steep climb in global demand for laptop computers, smart phones and everything else that assisted the consumer to be on-line at all times. The tech revolution created a huge demand for entirely new classes of consumer goods.
- *Higher demand for consumer goods in developed countries.* Beginning in the mid 1990s there began across much of the western world a period of unusually rapid increases in house prices. This rise brought with it a rising appetite for consumption – including for manufactured goods – on the part of the home owners.

China was granted entry into the World Trade Organisation in 2001. In that year, with rival countries laid low because of the Asian Crisis, it found itself almost alone on the world stage as a reliable, low cost manufacturing location in the midst of an unprecedented global surge in demand for low cost manufactured goods, and an increasingly liberal approach to trade in those goods.

In the years which followed, China's export trade, already very large, grew to massive proportions. By 2010 it seemed that the rest of the world had out-sourced its manufacturing to China. To give some statistics, in 2010 China produced:

- One in every six of the world's motor cars.
- Two out of every three pairs of the world's shoes.
- Seven out of every ten of the world's mobile phones, which meant that Chinese factories produced 1.1 billion of them, up from 50 million in 2000.

- Eight out of every ten of the world's airconditioners, which came to a total of 109 million, up from the about 20 million which were made in China ten years earlier.
- Nine out of every ten computers manufactured on the planet. That came to a total of 360 million Made in China computers, up from less than 7 million in 2000.

This is just a sample. The ten years between 2000 and 2010 was a golden decade for China. With its cities adding 10% more floorspace each year, and its factory system growing even faster, the country developed a huge appetite for metals, minerals and energy.

The Price Hikes

This new demand quickly soaked up any spare mining and smelting capacity inside China. The tonnage of steel used inside China doubled between 1997 and 2003.[19] Even larger increases were seen in aluminium and copper. Over the same period, its annual consumption of coal rose by 500 million tonnes. China's miners, who struggled to keep up even in normal times, could not keep pace with this ferocious increase in demand. With their stockpiles nearly empty and furnaces in danger of shutting down, the country's smelters had no choice but to turn to the outside world for help.

At this point it is worth noting that, in the early 2000s, there were two quite distinct worlds in global mining. There were the hard-pressed Chinese miners, struggling to keep up with galloping demand. Then there were the hard-pressed miners everywhere else, struggling to stay profitable in the face of ever-declining prices. For a decade the two worlds had existed side-by-side, not greatly impacting on each other. For western miners, sales to China were a welcome bonus, a sideshow to the main game.

When the Chinese smelters turned to the outside world, they were no doubt welcomed with open arms, but for a while they were still treated as a sideshow. That attitude began to change when shipments to China swelled to the point where they started to soak up the excess supply in global markets. This had become a real factor by the end of 2002 but the noise of day-to-day events was masking it. One senior mining executive who was more familiar than most with the state of mining across the globe said in early 2003: "Last year was one of pervasive weakness in commodity prices… [this was due to] sluggish economic activity in the countries of our major customers, with the exception of China." China rated a mention, but not much more than that.

A few months later it was rating more than just a mention. China was the central topic of discussion at Toronto's Prospectors and Developers Conference in April 2003. It was obvious that it was becoming more important in global markets. Instead of importing about 6% of the outside world's copper, as had long been the case, the country was now importing 20%. The question at the conference was: how important would it become? The general view was neatly expressed by one conference presenter: "There is some doubt whether China can continue its rapid growth."

The doubters were reducing in number by the end of 2003, by which time there had been a considerable tightening of global supply, all of it due to China's growing demands. Metal prices were shifting upwards. Then about halfway through the next year the realisation suddenly dawned that global supply was no longer just tightening, it had become very tight. With that realisation, prices leapt upwards. The copper price went up by 50% over the course of 2004, and nickel jumped by 40%. Steel went up 30% and aluminium 20%. The coal index rose by 65%. Held back by its unusual pricing mechanism, iron ore managed only a 20% rise in 2004. The next year it rose by 70%. With iron ore prices practically doubling in just two years, the China mining boom had begun.[20]

The prices kept rising through 2005, 2006 and 2007. By the end of 2007, copper and zinc prices had increased by two and a half times since the China boom began and were at levels not seen since the headiest years of the 1950s and 60s. Iron ore and lead prices were not far behind. Steel and aluminium had also registered substantial increases, they were up by more than half since 2003, big jumps for metals which typically did not show a lot of price volatility. Even cement, which could be called the strong, silent type of the mineral sector, saw its price rise by nearly 25%. For cement, a rise of that magnitude was verging on the revolutionary.

They were good times for the mining companies. The biggest of them – BHP Billiton and Rio Tinto – began reporting profits of US$5 billion and more.[21] They climbed into the ranks of the most profitable companies on earth.

The prices reached in 2007 were for most minerals and metals about as good as they got. Things settled down a bit after that. Then along came the Global Financial Crisis, slowing industrial activity and creating excess mineral supply for the first time in years. Sharp price drops followed. They then rebounded equally sharply when the Chinese government put its stimulus program into action. Actually, they not only rebounded, in some cases they shot past the already high levels of 2007. The copper price was one such case. Having reached US$7,700 per tonne in 2007 it hit nearly US$10,000 in early 2011. That was not sustained for long. It was falling again the following year and had, by 2014, returned to the levels reached in 2007. Most other benchmark prices did the same.

The major exception to that was iron ore. The price it reached in 2007 was just the beginning. In that year, the Japanese cartel was still in control. After being forced into allowing a 70% price rise in 2005, the cartel had rallied and pulled off the impressive feat of keeping the price rise to 20% in 2006 and 10% in 2007. The image comes to mind of a slightly-built person attempting to restrain an over-sized Great Dane from chasing after a cat. By 2007 the iron ore producers were straining on the leash, and the Japanese were struggling to control them. They were not strong enough. Prices jumped 65% in 2008. Then in 2009 the iron ore producers slipped the leash altogether. The annual pricing negotiations broke down and were replaced by spot pricing. Prices soared. The benchmark price reached US$168 per tonne in December 2010, up from US$14 in 2003. It was a rise of over 1,000%.

The Chinese Response

The mining boom is best known outside China for the great surge in the prices of many of the ores which were shipped to China from mines around the world. This may produce in the mind's eye an image of rows of smoke-belching Chinese smelters fed with expensive foreign ores and coal. This image captures part of the reality, but it is far from conveying the full picture. Because a large proportion of the feed to the Chinese smelters came from its domestic mines. During the mining boom, China was the largest and most active mining nation in the world.

Take copper as an example. Production from China's mines doubled over the decade, while outside China it rose by a mere 25%. It was a similar story in bauxite where Chinese domestic output grew nearly fivefold over the decade, while in the rest of the world it rose by 50%. And in coal, total tonnes produced per year in China rose by two and half times over the decade, while all the other countries on earth, taken together, could only manage a 25% increase. Even in iron ore, the wider world's best performing sector, China did better. In the outside world, production of iron units nearly doubled, in China it tripled over the decade.

It is not as though China was starting from a low base. It was already the leading mining country in the world. Yet in each of these sectors, the country's rate of expansion was either the highest, or second highest, of any major producing country. To put it another way: during the mining boom, China out-performed every other nation on earth when it came to digging ore out of the ground.

It did even better in the refining and smelting of ores. Not only was its growth in smelting capacity extremely rapid, the sheer scale of it was far in excess of anything seen before. Consider the case of steel. It had taken nearly fifty years to install China's first 100 million tonnes of steel making capacity. In the ten years of the mining boom another 500 million tonnes was built. Even at the height of their industrialisation, neither the United States, Japan nor the Soviet

Union ever came close to this adding this sort of capacity. In fact, all three of them combined did not even come close.

All of this raises the question: how did China build so much mining and smelting capacity so quickly? There is a two-pronged answer to that. Firstly, China had the greatest incentive to do it and the most motivated group of business people with which to make it happen. Secondly, China could bring projects, large and small, into production in far less time than it took in more established mining countries.

The second part of that answer warrants a closer look. Projects in China fell into two broad categories: large and small. The large projects were mostly the responsibility of the larger state-owned enterprises, and were approved by the central government in Beijing. The small projects were privately-owned or run by the smaller state-owned enterprises. These were approved at the provincial or, more commonly, the municipal level.

Each smelting sector was comprised of such large and small projects. In each sector there were typically ten or a dozen large complexes of national importance, and then was long tail of smaller ones, right down to the very small.

It was different in the mining sectors. Their industry structure depended on the nature of the orebodies. In bauxite, the bulk of domestic Chinese production came from four large complexes of deposits. In copper, there were three large centres and many small ones. In iron ore, small mines abounded. There were 8,000 of them in operation in 2007. A few were fairly large but most were minnows, of a size which would not have attracted a second glance from a western miner. Many were even smaller than that. Coal was a mixture of large and small. About half of the country's output came from mines with a capacity above one million tonnes per year, a good size by global standards. At the other end of the scale, between one quarter and one third of production came from small underground workings which were operated with little expertise and the most basic of equipment.

Returning to the question of how China managed to build its mining and smelting production base so rapidly during the mining boom, it is best to start by looking at the large-scale plants. The reason they could be built with the speed that they achieved was due to two things: very fast project approval processes, and very fast project construction.

The speed of project approval in any country depends on how quickly (a) the Board of a company will grant approval and (b) the regulatory authorities will grant approval. In China the Board approval process was often very fast because bringing on new production capacity for building materials was a low risk undertaking. Urban construction was going at full speed and future sales were almost assured. The economy was so large that even half a dozen major projects in the same sector could be commenced at the same time without fear that they would add too much capacity. Which meant that the Boards of Chinese companies typically did not have the long internal debates, market studies and options consideration which were common in western countries. As long as the project looked like it would make money, it got the tick of approval.

As for regulatory approval, China had, in practice if not in law, the least stringent processes in the world. The Chinese authorities were pro-business at every level. Everyone's aim was to help build a plant which increased production of something. If that project also caused some environmental damage, that was unfortunate but a consequence which could be lived with. Most projects got the tick of approval without too much scrutiny.

As for how the speed of construction was so rapid once the approval was granted, there were two factors at work. Firstly, there were few frills with Chinese mines and industrial plants, even the large ones. Designs which were borrowed from another project were often deemed good enough. Secondly, these designs were then constructed around the clock, six or even seven days a week, with nearly as many labourers on-site at midnight as there were at midday.[22] The overall result was that large projects could be brought on-stream in under two years if they involved a simple design like an aluminium smelter. A more complex development took a bit longer.

As for the small projects, they could be built in less than a year. They used "cookie cutter" designs[23] handed from one to another, incorporating cheap machinery, with little in the way of equipment to promote efficiency, safety or pollution control. They were waved through the approval process, if there was one, with little scrutiny. Dozens of them could be brought on-stream every couple of years. In coal, towards the end of the decade, a small mine was being commissioned every week.

The biggest production base of steel mills, aluminium smelters and copper refineries came into being in the triangle formed by Liaoning, Shandong and Shanxi provinces.[24] This region was also home to the country's main concentration of coal and iron ore mines as well as the "northern system" of China's bauxite production base.

It is truly remarkable how quickly this production base was built and expanded. To give some illustration of the speed and scale of developments in this region, in the three years between 2004 and 2007, the capacity of copper refining in Shandong province grew from zero (there were no refineries at all in 2004) to 10% of the world's capacity. In just those three years, four large smelting and refining complexes, all fed by imported ores, were constructed and commissioned. The capacity built during that time equalled that of the entire Japanese sector, a longstanding and important one in the global scene.

The Liaoning-Shanxi-Shandong triangle was also home to a huge expansion of the aluminium sector. China's aluminium smelting capacity, already the largest in the world, doubled between 2004 and 2007, and many of the new plants were built in Shandong and neighbouring Henan province. As for the country's alumina refining capacity, it tripled in size in those three years, with most of the new plants being built in the same region. In steel it was the same story. Coking coal deposits were found in the triangle, as were the majority of China's iron ore resources. Being also close to the iron ore importing ports, the triangle was home to more than half of China's steel production capacity. Over 100 million tonnes of steelmaking capacity – about the same as the entire Japanese industry – was built in just four years.

A second centre of metallurgical expansion – mainly in the steel and copper sectors – was in Shanghai and its adjoining provinces, Jiangsu and Anhui. Iron ore and coal – both foreign and domestic – was unloaded at Ningbo and the other bulk handling ports of the region and railed or barged up the Yangtze river to where it was needed. The hinterland of Shanghai became home to China's second main concentration of copper smelters and refineries. They were fed with imported concentrates and also with ores mined in China's oldest copper region, where Anhui, Hubei and Jiangxi provinces came together. Copper refining capacity in the area nearly doubled between 2004 and 2007, to the point where it was almost 10% of global capacity in just this region alone.

China's third main concentration of smelting complexes was in Sichuan province, in the south-eastern part of China. Steel and aluminium were the main metallurgical industries, feeding off the iron ore and bauxite reserves found nearby. It was an area long known to be rich in minerals. During the period 2003 to 2007 steel output tripled, and aluminium rose fourfold.

Throughout the mining boom China's construction of smelting and refining capacity was so rapid that, instead of having to encourage it, the central government put considerable effort into slowing it down. Periodically it would order a "chopping of the tail", or the closure of plants below a certain size. It also issued regulations insisting on minimum sizes for new plants, banning particular inefficient technologies and, for some sectors, insisting on a certain proportion of domestically mined feed. The aim was to prevent overcapacity, encourage domestic mine development and, especially, to reduce waste and pollution. Such measures usually had some effect, but there were many ways to get around them, including by ignoring them outright. So despite the government's periodic efforts, the sprawling, chaotic, breakneck expansion of Chinese industry created an environmental mess.[25]

Chapter 3

THE IMPACT ON GLOBAL MINING

The great surge in China's smelting capacity far-outstripped the ability of its domestic mines to feed them. Foreign ores were needed in huge tonnages. It might be expected that all the world's mining regions would have risen to the challenge when presented with a once-in-a-lifetime opportunity like this. And, overall, global production did increase at a rapid rate, in many sectors at least. Global cement production grew at nearly 8% per year between 2004 and 2014. Steel, aluminium and nickel grew at 6%, coal at nearly 5% and lead and zinc at about 4%.

But most of it came from China and one or two other countries in each sector. It has to be said that, outside of China, the production response was (with notable exceptions) far short of what was needed or what might have been expected. In one important sector – mined copper – the entire global production response was nowhere near enough to satisfy the increased demand. In this chapter will be examined the response of global miners in four important sectors: mined copper, bauxite, coal and iron ore.

Mined Copper

Perhaps the oddest outcome of the mining boom was that, throughout it, global mined copper production grew at just 2.3% per year. This was at a time when underlying demand for copper was growing at 6% per year or even more. The supply of copper was so far from meeting demand that copper-deprived consumers were forced to turn to aluminium (to replace copper in electrical applications) and polycarbonate tubing (to replace copper in plumbing applications).[26] In the face of the greatest sustained rise in demand in 50 years, the world's copper producers went missing. What happened?

To get a better fix on this, it is useful to look at the issue on a regional basis. There are six main geographical regions for copper production. They are, in order of their size in 2003: South America, North America, the South Pacific, Greater Europe, China and Sub-Saharan Africa. During the mining boom these six regions fell into two groups. China and Sub-Saharan Africa formed the "frantic growth" group. The rest of the world formed what could be called the "stalled" group. In the frantic growth group, the rate of production increase between 2004 and 2014 was 6% per year. In the stalled group it was 1% per year. It was a stark contrast. During the previous 40 years, the stalled group had shown a consistent expansion rate of about 3%. Why did production growth in those regions nearly come to a halt during the mining boom?

Looking at North America first, growth did not in fact nearly come to a halt during the mining boom. It had come fully to a halt decades before that. Put simply, North American copper was a mature field. Three quarters of the output still came from mines which were opened before 1920. The three biggest of them were Morenci and Kennecott in the United States, and Buenavista in Mexico. Buenavista was opened in 1899, Kennecott in 1895 and Morenci in 1872.[27] With these three geriatric operations dominating the scene, overall production from the region had not really moved since the 1970s. The same could be said about Greater Europe. These two once-great regions had been more or less treading water since the 1970s. It is no surprise that that state of affairs continued through the mining boom.

It was more of a surprise that the Andes and the South Pacific were also in the stalled group. After all, these regions had driven growth in global copper production since the 1960s. Together they had added 90% of the world's increase between 1970 and 2000. Yet during the mining boom output growth from both regions nearly came to a halt. Why? Taking the Andes first, there were three reasons: (1) most of the good orebodies were already in production (2) the costs of developing new mines became prohibitive, and (3) mined head grades fell off a cliff.[28]

The decade of the 1990s had seen plenty of new capacity brought on-stream in Chile. The projects chosen for development were the best of a much larger group. They were the highest grade, with their ores closest to the surface, with the lowest level of troublesome impurities and requiring the least amount of infrastructure development. The deposits which had not been developed in the 1990s had been passed over for a reason. They were much less attractive. Each had some combination of lower grade, smaller size, deeper ore, major infrastructure requirements and elevated levels of arsenic and other nasty elements.

It did not help that the cost of developing those mines had gone sky-high. The mining boom had driven equipment costs far above historical levels. In one instance, a mine development which had been budgeted to cost US$1 billion in 2003 had risen to US$5 billion by 2011. Then there was the rising cost of labour. Labour strikes were common as workers observed the high prices of copper and wanted some for themselves. The Andean mine developments, already very expensive, became much more so during the mining boom.

But unattractive projects and high costs of construction did not stop mine development in its tracks. In fact, a good number of Andean mines were brought into production during the mining boom. The Spence project came on-stream in 2007, followed the next year by Codelco's Gabriela Mistral. Esperanza started-up in 2010. Then came a trio of new Chilean mines in 2013, one of which was the arsenic-laden Alejandro Hales. Toromocho, the sole Peruvian new mine development of the period, came on-stream right at the end, in 2014. There were also five major mine expansions, plus many smaller expansions and debottlenecking exercises. Four of the major ones were in Chile, at Escondida, Collahuasi, Andina and Los Bronces. The fifth was in Peru, at the Cerro Verde mine. Yet these many expansions hardly moved the dial on Andean copper production.

This is because head grades were falling so fast that the new production capacity served only to off-set it. In Chile the average mined head grade fell from 1.1% in 2003 to 0.7% in 2008. The decline slowed after that, but the damage was done. The impact was that, in 2008, three tonnes of copper ore had to be mined, moved and processed in order to achieve what only two tonnes could achieve just five years earlier. In other words, during the mining boom, the Andean mines had to increase their capacity by 50% just to stay still.

Turning to the South Pacific, that region, like the Andes, had seen very strong growth in production from the 1960s through to the early 2000s, and especially in the 1990s. During that decade, the Grasberg deposit on the island of Papua went from a fledgling producer to one of the biggest mines in the world, and in Australia, several large discoveries in the 1970s and 80s – one of them being Olympic Dam – were brought into full production.

When it came to the mining boom years, however, all of those expansion opportunities were gone. Added to that was the fact that the two biggest Papuan mines – Grasberg and OK Tedi – experienced major declines in production due to operational difficulties, mine disasters and political intervention. The result was that copper output from the island of Papua was cut in half over the decade, and output from the South Pacific region as a whole fell by one quarter.

So there it was. The regions which had propelled global production for the past forty years were either stalled or in decline because of worsening mining conditions (the Andes), lack of new projects (Australia) or operational and political strife (Papua). In the face of the resultant shortage, China was ransacked for anything resembling a near-to-surface copper deposit. The copper price was, after all, high enough to justify exploiting even the lowest of grades. The production centres in Jiangxi, Gansu and Yunnan were pushed for all they were worth.

A surprising amount of success was achieved by this brownfields-focussed, leave-no-stone-unturned approach. By 2008, mined copper production in China had reached one million tonnes per year. Six years later it exceeded 1.7 million tonnes and China had become the world's second ranked producing country. Still it was not enough to compensate for the loss of the growth from the Andes and South Pacific. In fact, it was nowhere near enough.

Which is why the nearly forgotten fields of central Africa returned to centre stage. The Copperbelt, as these fields were known, had a long history.[29] Copper was discovered in this remote region by colonial explorers in the 1880s. The deposits were located in the Katanga province of what was then the Belgian Congo. The first large-scale production was begun in 1906 by Union Miniere du Haute Katanga (United Mines of Upper Katanga), a Belgian state-owned company. The Benguela railroad reached the area in 1911, linking it with the Angolan port of Lobito, nearly 2,000 kilometres away on the Atlantic coast. A lot of money was invested and, by the 1930s, the Copperbelt, which by then extended south across the border into neighbouring Rhodesia, had grown to become one of four centres of global production along with the western states of the USA, the Sudbury Basin in Canada and the Chilean Andes.

The region had retained its global importance through the 1940s and 50s, and even through the strife-torn decades of the 1960s and 1970s. The Belgians withdrew from the Congo in 1960, and the Republic of the Congo was created. The British withdrew from Northern Rhodesia four years later, creating the Republic of Zambia. The Zambian transition was peaceful enough but in the Congo it was not. There was a two-year civil war which ended in General Mobutu seizing power. He would later re-name the country Zaire.

Mobutu closed down Union Miniere and replaced it with the new state-owned company, Gecamines. Not to be outdone, in Zambia, President Kaunda also nationalised the copper mines, creating Zambian Consolidated Copper Mines, or ZCCM.[30] In the 1970s, another post-independence struggle impacted the region. It happened when civil war erupted in Angola, destroying the Benguela railroad and forcing Gecamines and ZCCM to use trucks to shift their smelted copper south to ports in South Africa. Through it all production continued, largely unaffected. The period between 1960 and the 1980 saw the Copperbelt producing at about 1.1 million tonnes per year, not all that far behind the Andes.

Like much of the rest of the economy of Africa, serious decline began in the Copperbelt in the 1980s. It got worse in the 1990s. On the Zairean side, civil conflict engulfed the region when the aging and terminally corrupt President Mobutu could no longer contain his rivals. Armed challenges to his regime gathered strength and this time the copper mines could not avoid the trouble. They had virtually closed down by 1993. Four years later Mobutu fled, seeing out his days in Morocco. With him gone, the country got its third name in forty years. It was renamed the Democratic Republic of the Congo, or DRC.

On the Zambian side, the mines also ran into trouble, although more gradually. The trouble there was ineffective management and under-investment by the cash-strapped government. So it was that, by the end of the 1990s, the Zambian mines were treading water and the DRC mines were barely operating at all. The once-thriving Copperbelt was a backwater in international copper.

The Copperbelt might have been down on its luck, but it remained a potential powerhouse. Its luck turned for the better when the price of copper started to climb in 2004. Picture the situation: in a remote but well-trodden part of central Africa there were eight or ten already-known world-class copper orebodies, close to the surface, with high grades and carrying plenty of by-product cobalt. Some of the orebodies were in production although not well run, others had once been producing mines and were now shuttered, and still others had been studied in detail over the years but never entered production. All they needed was money, good management and a few years.

In fact the money and good management had never been far away. The Toronto-based First Quantum had taken a stake in the region as far back as 1996, acquiring the Bwana Mkubwa mine, once the jewel in the crown of the Copperbelt. Glencore was also active before the mining boom, as was Phelps Dodge. These companies and others were well-positioned to ramp-up production when the time came. So when the copper price went up, ZCCM and Gecamines were only too happy to take their free carry and step aside. Two big mines, Kansanshi and Tenke Fungurume, were up and running by 2005 and 2009 respectively. The Copperbelt had twenty active mines by 2012.

Chinese state-owned enterprises were also involved in the revival of the Copperbelt. As part of China's global mineral supply strategy, China Non-Ferrous Metal Mining Company had bought the Chambishi mine in Zambia in 1998.[31] Chinese companies missed out in the 2004-06 rush to buy the Copperbelt's largest orebodies, so they took stakes in the smaller ones. Several Chinese construction companies worked a different angle, they struck deals with the governments of the Zambia and the DRC to provide infrastructure, with part of their return being favoured access to undeveloped deposits.

With all this foreign investment, the DRC mines went in ten years from producing almost nothing to producing over one million tonnes per year. In neighbouring Zambia, output more than doubled. Without this revival of the Copperbelt, China would have been the sole engine of global copper production during the mining boom.

Bauxite

In contrast to the situation in copper, there was never any shortage of aluminium during the mining boom. If anything, there was an oversupply. But there was at least one similarity between copper and bauxite. In both sectors, the established mining regions in the western world failed to respond fast enough to feed China's smelters.

Again, the numbers help to illustrate the issue. During the mining boom, global bauxite production rose from an annual production of 170 million tonnes in 2004 to 300 million tonnes in 2014. Of this additional 130 million tonnes, some was produced in India and consumed in Indian smelters. Nearly all of the rest of it was fed into Chinese smelters. And three quarters of that came from Chinese mines or from newly-developed Indonesian bauxite pits located in coastal areas in the southern half the island of Borneo. Bauxite mines in the rest of the world accounted for a mere quarter of the total global increase.

To get a better handle on this, it is useful to break down global bauxite production into its major regions. In 2002, just a year or so before the mining boom began, four fifths of the world's non-Chinese bauxite came from only four countries. Australia was by far the largest, accounting for nearly half of the world's bauxite production outside China. Then came Guinea in West Africa, Brazil and Jamaica.

These four had dominated global bauxite for decades. Jamaica had been an important producing region since the 1950s, Guinea since the '60s and Australia since the '70s.[32] Brazil was the new kid on the block, having become a significant producer during the 1990s.

The next step in the production chain – the refining of bauxite into alumina – was often done near to where it was produced but this was far from a standard practice. It was equally common for the alumina refineries to be built in locations which were close to sources of cheap natural gas and also close to a port capable of unloading ocean-going vessels carrying bulk loads. In 2002, the main producing countries for alumina were the United States, Australia, Brazil and Jamaica.

As for smelting, it was mostly done in the countries where the aluminium was consumed. For this reason, China, in 2002, had the world's largest aluminium smelting capacity. It had a bauxite and alumina production base capable of supplying about half of its feedstock. The rest had to be imported, and in 2002 that meant shipping in, for the most part, Australian alumina.

With this significant deficit in locally-produced alumina, when the mining boom began, Chinese smelter owners mounted a global search for new supplies. But, as they searched, Chinese industry leaders realised that it would be much quicker and cheaper to build their own alumina refining capacity and develop their own new mining capacity. So began a rush to build China-based refineries and open Chinese domestic mines.

The country's alumina output doubled between 2004 and 2006, and then it doubled again by 2008. In a single year, 2006, a dozen large refineries were brought into production. In 2004 China had ranked a distant second, well behind Australia, as a refiner of alumina. By 2007 it was the world leader.

China's bauxite production did not quite follow at the same pace because its resource base was not large enough. But a great effort was put into developing the domestic deposits. Development times were far quicker than elsewhere. A greenfields mine development was sometimes in production just 12 months after construction began. Domestic bauxite production doubled in the first four years of the mining boom.

But even that was not enough, so the Chinese turned to foreign sources. They had no luck in Jamaica. That long-established production base was already in decline and was hard-pressed just to sustain current output. They had no luck in Guinea either. The country's main mine, Sangaredi,[33] was already at full capacity, and the corrupt and uncooperative political situation meant that there was little appetite for further investment. In Australia and Brazil the Chinese encountered a more positive response, and the production systems in both countries were pushed harder.

But in both countries, especially Australia, there was a reluctance to commit to new mine capacity. Indeed, in all the world's established bauxite fields only two new mines were brought into production during the mining boom. Both were in Brazil. One of them was

CVRD's majority-owned Paragominas, located in Para State. The other was Alcoa's Juruti project, also in Para State. The reluctance to build new mines was due in part to a lack of good options. It was also due to the fact that the price for bauxite was not rising by very much. This was because a steadily swelling river of bauxite was flowing out of previously little-noticed fields in Indonesia and filling the gaps in the market as soon as they opened up.

Chinese traders had for years purchased bauxite from small local companies digging these Indonesian fields. It was good quality mineral if a bit low in actual aluminium content. When the mining boom began, the trade increased. Then, as the pressure grew to feed China's proliferating alumina refineries, it began to ramp-up rather quickly. One particular focal point was the islands of the Riau Archipelago, which formed a series of stepping stones stretching from Sarawak on Borneo to southern Malaysia. Bauxite mining on Riau developed exceptionally rapidly, almost in gold rush style. Hundreds of small producers, typically working with the bare minimum of equipment and permits, sprang into life using cheap labour drafted in from Indonesia's overcrowded cities. When those fields were full, the bauxite-rush spread to West Kalimantan, one of four Indonesian provinces on the island of Borneo. It too soon became a thriving field.

From producing maybe 5 million tonnes per year at the start of the mining boom, just four years later Indonesia was providing half of China's imports.[34] As still more Chinese alumina refining capacity came on-stream, the deposits of West Kalimantan were brought into more organised production. The biggest mine on the field, Tangerang, was the largest bauxite mine which came into production during the mining boom anywhere in the world. Its entire output was shipped as raw mineral to China.

The Indonesian fields were an easily accessible and low-cost source for the Chinese, and they were exploited to the full. The rate of growth was extraordinary. Having been almost unknown in global bauxite in 2004, by 2011 Indonesia was ranked third in the world for bauxite production, behind only Australia and China. The whole field had been developed with a minimum of capital investment, taking advantage of the fact that the mineral was close to the surface, easy to dig using front-end loaders, and could be readily transported using 50-tonne dump trucks to local ports. It was perfectly suited to the Chinese style of rapid, no-frills development with the single aim of producing great tonnages as quickly and cheaply as possible.

But many in the Indonesian government were unimpressed with this state of affairs, and the Kalimantan bauxite fields were closed in 2013.[35] It is worth dwelling for a moment on their closure because it was the clearest expression of resource nationalism made during the mining boom. In mineral exporting countries the argument is sometimes made that exporting the nation's mineral wealth is akin to squandering the national birth right. This argument has always been potent in Indonesia, as it has in India. During the mining boom, the argument became particularly potent. Especially when Indonesians stood by watching as half of the world's exported bauxite departed their shores to feed the aluminium production complex in China, while in Indonesia there was only a small and aging aluminium smelter, and no alumina refining capacity whatsoever.

To the lawmakers in Jakarta this spectacle made it appear as though Indonesia was just a servant of the Chinese. It was not just in bauxite. A similar situation existed in coal, copper and nickel. In each case, Indonesia was home to some of the world's largest resource bases, but processed or used only a fraction of it.

It is true that many other countries followed this model of exporting barely-processed minerals in large tonnages. Two examples were world leading mineral producers: Australia in iron ore and Chile in copper. But in Indonesia there was a lot of unhappiness about it. This finally found its expression in law when it was decreed that all Indonesian minerals would be smelted, or at least further processed, inside Indonesia. The law became effective on January 12, 2014. It brought Kalimantan exports of bauxite to a near complete halt. It was a shock to the global system.

In response to the shock the traders fanned out again. Twelve months later a completely new bauxite field had sprung up to replace it. It was near the city of Kuantan on the east coast of the Malaysian peninsular. A Riau Islands-style development, within two years it was producing at the level of the Indonesian fields at their peak.

This is how the supply of bauxite to China was delivered for most of the mining boom. Chinese domestic mines were supported by the opportunistically-developed Indonesian and then Malaysian fields, which in turn were supplemented by much more capital-intensive mines in Brazil and Australia. As it had in copper, this dynamic highlighted the weakness of the world's existing production platform. It was slow to respond, and indeed had limited capacity to respond, when a sharp rise in demand placed pressure on the system.

Coal

Being home to a bauxite sector which rose from nothing to be the major source of China's imports makes Indonesia one of the key countries of the mining boom. But its contribution did not stop there. It played a very similar role in global coal.

When the mining boom began, China was an important exporter of coal. That China should export its coal had long been an objective of the Chinese leadership. As far back as 1980, Deng Xiaoping had pushed for development of the coalfields and for the construction of a dedicated coal transport corridor from Shanxi to the export ports on the coast. Accordingly, a railway had been built, joining the Datong coalfields to Qinhuangdao,[36] a port located on the Bohai Sea, not all that far from Beijing. Export shipments reached ten million tonnes per year in late 1980s. But there was a lot more than ten million tonnes of coal passing through the port. The majority of it was not actually exported, instead it was loaded onto bulk carriers which made their way south to be unloaded at Shanghai, Guangdong and other coastal cities.

As the Chinese economy grew, so too did the traffic along this corridor. As a result, it was constantly congested, so other railways and ports were constructed. The coastal coal traffic grew in size. So too did coal exports such that, by 2001, China was shipping over 100 million tonnes per year to other Asian nations, especially Japan and South Korea. It ranked second in the world as an exporter, behind only Australia which was by far the largest coal exporting nation.

China's rising prominence in export markets went into reverse when the mining boom began, because its domestic coal consumption began to climb ever faster. To put this in numbers: in the first five years of the boom, the Chinese domestic consumption of coal increased at over 200 million tonnes per year. This remarkable rate of growth was marched by an equally remarkable achievement: China's domestic coal mining base was expanded so fast that it could actually keep pace with this demand.[37] But the railways, despite heroic efforts to improve haulage efficiency, could not keep up. The result was a slow erosion of the export trade. This is because the coal was more needed in the cities of the Yangtze or Pearl River Deltas than in Seoul or Tokyo. The year 2001 was the high point of China's coal exports. By 2008 they had dwindled to nothing. The next year, China became a net coal importer. Six years later, those imports were nearly 300 million tonnes.

It is important keep that in perspective. Imports of 300 million tonnes per year sounds like a lot. Indeed, it is a lot. Japan had no domestic coal to speak of and even it was not importing that much. But for China, the coal imports never became more than a top-up. Its domestic coal production was ten times the tonnage of its imports. Right through the mining boom, the country's coal production base continued to expand at an almost reckless rate. In 2014, it produced 3.6 billion tonnes. It was almost half of the entire world's production.

At this point it is necessary to draw the distinction between thermal and coking coal. China was throughout the mining boom the world's largest producer of both thermal coal and coking coal. The thermal coal was for use in its power plants, and the coking coal for use in its blast furnaces and other industrial applications. China imported almost nothing of either for the first half of the mining boom. Then during the second half, as its transport system could no longer keep pace, it became the largest importer of both.

This alone put plenty of pressure on coal producers in the exporting countries. But there was more to come. Because, as it turned out, China was not the only country to greatly increase its thermal and coking coal imports during the mining boom. India was the other.

In 2004, India was third ranked in the world in both the production of coal and its consumption. Like China, India has very large and accessible coal deposits. However, unlike China, which has very good quality coal deposits, Indian coal tends to be of poor quality.[36] It contains high levels of those chemicals which create problems when the coal is burnt. Not only that, Indian coal is almost all of the thermal variety. The coking coal deposits which are widely found in China are almost absent in India. The internal transport of coal is also a problem. The railways are constantly jam-packed, because Indian governments have always been slow to build infrastructure, especially of the type that uses a lot of land.

For all these reasons – poor quality thermal coal, an absence of coking coal and the difficulty of sending it by rail from mine to mill – India, despite its large coal reserves, imported 30 million tonnes in 2004. That was already enough to put it well into the top ten importing countries. However, it is what happened during the next ten years that really had an impact on global markets. Because in 2014, India imported 260 million tonnes. Which meant that in the ten years after 2004, India's total imports of coal rose to be nearly as much as China's.

There were two drivers of this. The first was the country's growing need for energy. The Indian economy had been developing at a fast pace since its markets had been opened to foreign trade in the early 1990s. By the time the mining boom began, it was about at the stage where the Chinese economy was in 1980. That meant the next ten years were a period of rapidly growing demand for electricity, cement, steel and aluminium with the result that India embarked on a nationwide program of power station construction. Coal consumption doubled during the ten years of the mining boom. Nearly all the coking coal had to be imported.

The second driver of Indian coal imports was the need to alleviate India's urban pollution which grew worse as the mining boom years wore on. The smog which blanketed major cities including Delhi, Mumbai and Chennai was a strong driver to action.[38] Part of the solution was the importing of higher quality thermal coal from Australia and especially Indonesia. In this way, India went from importing about one in every fourteen tonnes of the coal it consumed in 2004, to importing about one in every four tonnes in 2014.

Taken together, China and India drove the global coal trade to heights never before seen. Where during the 1990s, and even during the first half of the 2000s, Japan was the dominant force in the coal market, by the end of the mining boom it was a second-string player. By 2014, China was importing almost three times as much as Japan. So was India.

Where did all the coal come from? The short answer is that, in coking coal, Australia was, and remained, the main supplier. In thermal coal, most of new export supply came from Indonesia. It was produced in a chaotic scramble in much the same way as its bauxite.

The Indonesian coal rush, as it might be called, began in earnest when China became a net importer of thermal coal. In response, Chinese traders did what they did best: they spread out across the world looking for extra supplies. One obvious place to look was Australia. That country was the blue-chip supplier to the world. Its mines were large and could supply good quality consistently. That made them the preferred supplier for the Japanese, Taiwanese and Koreans, all of whom wanted long-term contracts and predictable quality well into the future.

The province of South Kalimantan was also an important producer and exporter of thermal coal to nearby Japan and Taiwan, but it had always played second fiddle to the Australians. This changed when the Chinese arrived. Japanese corporate executives and Chinese traders had a very different view on life. The Chinese were not too worried about the long-term future and they could even put up with indifferent quality. They just wanted more coal, preferably of the kind which could be mined cheaply and which did not need any expensive and hard-to-build infrastructure. The fields of Kalimantan and Sumatra were tailor-made for them.[39] They were extensive surface deposits for the most part, containing coal which was not world-beating but good enough. Because they were remote and mostly small, they were never suitable for the Japanese. Prior to the mining boom there really was no-one bothering to pursue them.

But the arrival of Chinese traders carrying rolls of cash changed everything. All of a sudden it was possible to make money from them. All the aspiring miner needed was a collection of diesel-fuelled front-end loaders, a small fleet of dump trucks and a good number of labourers. Of labourers, there was a huge reservoir in Indonesia's main cities. As for the loaders and trucks, they could be diverted from the neighbouring palm oil plantations or brought over from the cities.

And this is how the Kalimantan fields sprang into life. About half of the coal came from large, established producers already working the bigger deposits. The rest of it came from many hundreds of smaller, informal operations. In all, by 2009 there were a thousand or more coal producers of all sizes working the fields of Kalimantan and Sumatra.

This production system required very little by way of capital investment in infrastructure, or in mine development, and could be expanded very rapidly as long as the cheap labour kept coming in from the populous islands of Java and Sumatra and the coal was relatively accessible on the surface.

Turning now to coking coal, that Australia should become the world's main exporter of it during the mining boom was no surprise. After all, it had been the leading exporter since the 1980s,[40] supplying the baseload to the Japanese steelmills and then to Taiwan's China Steel and Korea's POSCO as they rose to join the ranks of the world's biggest steel makers.

The production base was located in two regions: the Bowen Basin in central Queensland, and the Hunter Valley, about two hours drive north of Sydney. When the mining boom began in 2004 and Chinese coal exports started to fall, the Asian buyers of the Chinese coal turned first to Australia. It caught them unawares, and for the next four years queues of bulk vessels, sometimes fifty or sixty long, bobbed up and down in waters outside the port of Newcastle and Hay Point waiting their turn at the coal loader. As for the miners, they also waited their turn to load their coal onto a train. The railway and port system was as jam-packed as in China or India.

The port and rail authorities' response to this was, to put it mildly, somewhat delayed. For the first three, even four, years of the mining boom, coal tonnages loaded in Australia's ports hardly increased at all. But when China's exports fell to nothing and it started looking for foreign coal, the port and rail systems were ready. The port of Newcastle was the most active, loading 150 million tonnes onto the bulk carriers in 2014 versus just 80 million in 2008.[41] The Bowen Basin ports were slower to act but shipments from there also rose substantially.

So it was that the global coal took on the same shape as global copper and bauxite. In each of these sectors, China led the way during the mining boom, helped along by easy-to-develop fields in parts of the world which had been deemed too politically risky or too small and patchy to be worth the investment. Then all of that was supplemented by the established miners. Not every mineral sector was like that. In iron ore, for example, it was the established miners who were the star of the show.

Iron Ore

As the mining boom began there were five main established iron ore producing regions in the outside-China world. They were the Pilbara in Western Australia, the "southern system" in Brazil's Minas Gerais State, the "northern system" in Para State, the aging Mesabi Range in Minnesota and the equally old and aging Krivoy Rog in the Ukraine.

India too was home to a sizeable iron ore sector. There were also some smaller fields in Russia and South Africa.

The Mesabi Range, Krivoy Rog and Russian mines were low grade, expensive, difficult to expand, far from any seaport and already over-committed just supplying their local steel industries. They played no part in supplying the Chinese steel industry during the mining boom. The Australian and Brazilian mines, on the other hand, had come into existence for the purpose of exporting to the Japanese, European and North American steel mills. They were large open-cut mines, high grade orebodies, cheap to operate, relatively easy to expand and connected to large bulk shiploading ports by well-built railways and pipelines. These two regions, especially the Pilbara, would by the end of the mining boom be the baseload suppliers to the Chinese mills.

A brief description of the Pilbara and the Brazilian fields will be useful. There was so much iron ore in the Pilbara that the mining of it was almost a secondary consideration.[42] The big issue in this region was not how to mine it but how to most effectively transport the ore from the remote inland mines to the customer steel mills which lay far across the ocean. The railway and port infrastructure was the bottleneck of the operations. Three groups of ports – Port Hedland, Dampier and Port Walcott – had been built in the 1960s and 70s, as had three railways which connected those ports to the mines. So central were these rail-port networks that, instead of being mining operations, the Pilbara operations were better described as transportation systems whose purpose was to load inland iron ore onto the world's ocean-going bulk cargo fleet.

In Brazil it was a similar story, with different details. The original iron ore mines, built largely in the 1960s, were still in full swing. They were located in the province of Minas Gerais, which lay inland from the cities of Rio de Janeiro and Sao Paulo. There were two types of ore in the Minas Gerais mines. One was high grade and required no processing. This was loaded onto railcars and hauled to coastal ports. Then there was the low grade ore which had first to be finely ground and treated to liberate the iron mineral. This ore, once treated, could be mixed with water and pumped through pipelines to the coast. There were two ports built for receiving the ores and loading them onto ocean-going vessels. The largest of them, Tubarao, was the largest bulk mineral loading port in the world. Its smaller cousin, Sepetiba, was further to the south, just outside Rio de Janeiro.

By the 1990s the mines of Minas Gerais were approaching the limits of their potential capacity. The scope for expanding the ports was also limited. So the decision had been made to build a new mine and transportation network. The mine would be built on the Carajas orebody, a huge and high grade deposit located in Para state, in Brazil's Amazon basin. Being in the north, this new centre of production was called the Northern System,[43] while the Minas Gerais operations were called the Southern System (later this was divided into Southern and South Eastern Systems). The Northern System was where the scope for future expansion was.

The Indian mines also deserve a mention, because they too played a part in the feeding of the Chinese steel mills. They could be grouped, like the Brazilian mines, into a southern system and a northern system. The southern system was located in the south-western States of Goa and Karnataka, where the export ports were Mormugao and Mangalore. The northern system was located in the north-eastern coastal state of Odisha and the two inland states adjoining it, Jharkand and Chhattisgarh. The main exporting ports serving this system were Paradip in the north, and Vishakhapatnam further south. At the beginning of the mining boom, the southern system was the larger producer but the expansion capability was with the northern system.

In the year 2000, if China is excluded, the Australian, Brazilian and Indian operations produced more than half of the world's iron ore. Nearly all of the Australian and Brazilian ore, and much of the Indian, was shipped to steel mills in Asia and Europe. Three companies – CVRD, Rio Tinto and BHP Billiton – dominated this trade. Forming a sort of Club of Three, for years they had carefully weighed any transport infrastructure and mine expansion projects, spending sometimes years in convincing the Japanese steel cartel of the wisdom of their proposals and then taking their deliberate time in the building stage. A major expansion of capacity was, in this orderly and slow-paced world, something of an event. India was also a player in this business but it was always a poor cousin. Its producing companies were too small, and the laws governing its mineral exports were too changeable, for them to be able to wield much influence.

When the China boom burst onto the international stage, these established producers found themselves in a new world. In just six months, from June to November 2004, demand rose so sharply that the approaches to the iron ore loading ports were obstructed by long queues of waiting vessels. Clearly, a great new opportunity faced the miners. To respond to it, the orderly, slow-moving Japanese-dominated world of the 1990s had to be left behind. The realisation began to dawn that there was no longer any need to seek the blessing of the Japanese cartel before something was done.

So the Club of Three, and the Indian suppliers, swung into action. BHP announced that it would be increasing its production capacity by half, Rio Tinto announced a doubling of capacity in its main shiploading ports and CVRD started ambitious expansion projects in both its northern and southern systems. For the next five years in Australia, Brazil and India there was continually evolving program of new mines, longer and double-tracked railways, innovative iron ore-conveying pipelines and larger ore loading ports. Approval and construction timetables shrank to a fraction of what they once had been. As importantly, and especially in India, more focussed rail and shiploading management ensured that the best use was made of existing capacity.

The result was that the three countries managed a combined iron ore output of 850 million tonnes in 2007, up from 520 million tonnes in 2003. In the Pilbara, exported tonnage rose from about 200 million tonnes to 300 million. It had taken fifteen years to go from 100 to 200 million tonnes. As for Brazil, its output rose from

230 million tonnes to 350 million. In India, the production increase was 100 million to 200 million tonnes per year, proportionally the best performance of all. That was no mean feat in a country with a fragmented and cash-strapped production base, severe transport congestion, byzantine approval processes and a political class which was instinctively opposed to exporting minerals.

The increases in the first five years of the boom took their toll in both Brazil and India. By 2007 their production systems were under stress. In Brazil, the Southern System had very little left to give. The ports at Itabira and Tubarao had been overloaded even before the China boom and after five years of putting further demands on them there were only a few minor expansion cards left to play. The Northern System, being comprised of the Carajas mine and the Madeira port, was difficult to expand. The Amazon Basin was continuing to resist all efforts to drive capacity additions. The main expansion prospect was Serra Sul, a Carajas-like orebody lying to the south of Carajas. The trouble was that Serra Sul was both a very expensive and a very contentious development. Even if it went according to plan it would not be in operation for another five years.

In India, the iron ore producers were fighting a losing battle. For one thing, there was never enough money for improving rail and port capacity. Added to that, mainly because of the innate distaste of Indian politicians for mineral exports, there was growing opposition to shipping iron ore to China. The trade was seen as undermining the future of the steel sector, and therefore undermining India's future economic growth potential. Things came to a head when in 2010 the Karnataka State government effectively put a halt to iron ore exporting.[44] Although the ban was lifted ten months later, it legitimised the anti-exports groups. This, in turn, led to the closure of many of the mines and raised taxes to the point where exports were unprofitable. By 2014, the Indian export iron ore trade had come to an almost complete halt.

The Chinese iron ore production base was also running into difficulties by 2007. It was completely out of high grade ore, and was rapidly depleting even its medium grade resources. Chinese iron ore had never been very good grade. For years the average iron content of the mined ore had been around 30%, about half the grade of the Australian variety. Now it was getting worse. In 2010, the average ore grade slipped to 25%, the next year it dropped to 20%. At that point it became closer to waste rock than ore. The Chinese responded by digging more of it out, but the best they could do was keep the total iron content produced steady year to year.

All of this meant that between 2008 and 2014 – in other words, for the rest of the mining boom period – there was no increase in either the total tonnage of iron ore production in Brazil, the total iron content produced in China, or the total ore available for export from India. Yet China's steel production was still climbing steeply. Between 2008 and 2014, it increased by a further 300 million tonnes. With the Brazilians stalled, the Indians opting out and China's domestic production dropping from exhaustion, where was the iron ore to come from?

It was at this critical point that the Pilbara production system showed just how much room for expansion it really had. Even after the first five years of rapid growth, Rio Tinto and BHP Billiton still had a range of options for big capacity additions. With high prices bringing in a fortune in profits, they also had the money to build the projects and bring them into production. Adding to this, the two incumbents had been joined by FMG, "the new force in iron ore". FMG was short for Fortescue Metals Group, a company which had been formed by the entrepreneurial Andrew Forrest.

FMG had been launched in 2003, just as the mining boom was starting. It had as its resource base several large iron ore deposits which had long been known about but ignored by Rio and BHP because they were lower grade ores, and as such deemed unacceptable by the Japanese steel mills. Forrest probably had a shrewd idea that the rules made by the Japanese cartel to determine what was acceptable quality ore were soon to be thrown out of the window. He no doubt also had a fair idea that China was soon to become the only market that really mattered. Which was good for him, because in the eyes of the Chinese, the FMG orebodies were just fine. Having secured the orebodies, all that Forrest needed was the rail and port.

He started by applying to share the existing transport infrastructure owned and operated by Rio and BHP. Such sharing arrangements were provided for under the terms of the decades-old operating leases agreed by the two companies with the State government. Still, it comes as no surprise that FMG's move was not welcomed by the two incumbents, and they mounted a strong resistance. A court battle ensued, which never came to a conclusion because the executives at FMG came to the realisation that sharing a rail and port was never going to work. So the company built, in just a few years, its own ore transport system, including a railway which ran parallel to BHP's for most of the way, and a new port in Port Hedland, where BHP's port had been built in the 1960s. The "new force in iron ore" loaded its first shipment in May 200847. The timing was perfect.

Through the remaining years of the mining boom these three Pilbara-based producers almost single-handedly drove the growth in global iron ore. Long-held assumptions about what could be achieved with the Pilbara's railways and ports fell by the wayside. Exports from the region more than doubled between 2009 and 2014. By the end of mining boom, the Pilbara was contributing about one in every two tonnes of the iron ore which was fed into China's blast furnaces.

Chapter 4

THE AFTERMATH

The Party Comes to an End

The Chinese economy was unstoppable in the first decade of the twentieth century. When an economy is performing in that way, it can seem as if the country's leadership has capabilities possessed by no-one else. They take on the air of financial wizards. But of course it is not the case. The extraordinary performance of the Chinese economy was always going to end.

In retrospect, the first signs of trouble appeared in 2006 when the economy was still going very strong. It was in that year that US house prices, having risen at about 10% per year since the late 1990s, started to fall. That was not supposed to happen. After all for the past seven years they had reliably gone up. The trend was such that US policymakers and everyone else had begun to assume that rising house prices were a permanent part of the economic landscape. Banks had started granting mortgages to people who obviously could not afford them. Their logic was that even if these financially-strapped new home owners did default, the bank's exposure would be minimal because in a few years the price of the house would have risen enough to cover them. The banks then packaged these mortgages into financial black boxes and sold them to other banks as low risk securities.

When house prices started to fall in 2006 it was seen as a minor correction. But they kept falling through 2007 and the level of concern started to grow. By mid 2008, with house prices still heading down, the banks started to take a closer look at their piles of "low risk" securities. They found that far from being low risk, they were of unknown risk, and quite possibly very high risk. When the reality of that sank in, there was a rush for the door. One thing led to another and by the end of 2008 global stock markets had lost 50% of their value. Many of the western countries sank into recession. It was called the Global Financial Crisis.

As recessions started to take hold in their customer countries, Chinese policymakers could see that income from their export trade was headed for a big fall. To consider what to do about it, a State Council meeting was held in early November 2008. The meeting ended with a dramatic decision: the Chinese government would pump $600 billion into the economy as a stimulus measure to replace the lost export revenue. Most of it went to some form or another of infrastructure spending.

It seemed to work. Unemployment in China barely rose at all, and the economy kept rolling along. Export shipments were down in 2009 but had recovered somewhat in 2010. They did not, however, bounce all the way back. By 2011 it was undeniable that the export engine of growth had slowed down. It was also clear that it was not solely due to the GFC. Two other factors were at work. Firstly, China's low-cost advantage was being eroded as average wages rose and rival countries entered the scene. Secondly, for the first time since Deng had come to power, there was serious political pushback in western countries against the ever-increasing in-flow of cheap Chinese manufactured goods.

The Chinese government had to respond. One way of doing that was to encourage greater consumer spending within China itself. But with all the economic uncertainty, and with their mortgages still to pay, the Chinese people were in saving mode not spending mode.

So with exports no longer growing and consumers unwilling to increase their spending, it was clear that some other engine of growth was needed for the economy. The engine to which the government turned was infrastructure spending. It had worked in 2009. For this reason, when the original $600 billion GFC stimulus package was spent, the government decided to keep it going. This time however, instead of making a big grant of taxpayer funds, the central government decided to make it easier for state-owned companies and municipal governments to borrow cheap money. The aim was the same: to create economic growth by giving easy money to state-owned companies and municipalities to spend on whatever projects they saw fit.

A second driver of the economy since 2010 has been the steady stream of rural migrants still coming into the cities. Although this flow of workers is no longer increasing, property developers have kept on building more apartments than they built the year before. The result is that residential construction typically runs well ahead of actual demand for apartments. The best illustration of this is the Ghost Cities. These are fully-constructed satellite cities complete with high rise apartment blocks and shopping malls, with no-one living in them. To date, experience shows that these apartments and shopping areas do in the end attract buyers and tenants. Even so, the Ghost Cities are one indication of how important a relentless, keep-on-building construction industry has become in the economy.

So it is that, spending on infrastructure and urban construction, funded by easy money, has been the main driver of Chinese economic growth since the GFC.[45] Infrastructure building has reached new heights. The national highway network has doubled in size in six years, and there has been a surge in railway and port construction the likes of which has never before been seen in China.

It keeps the economy ticking over at a good rate, but the best years are over. At least for now.

When the Dust Settled

In the first five years after the GFC, the impact of the Chinese government stimulus meant that the mining boom continued. But it couldn't last, and by 2014 the heat had undeniably come out of the global commodities markets. In that year, prices for coal, metals and ores had been flat or on a downward slope for a few years. The year 2014 is, therefore, as good a year as any to declare the end of the mining boom. Which means that it is also a good point at which to review how things had changed in the previous ten hectic years of global mining.

The biggest change was that an unprecedented concentration of global metal smelting capacity had been constructed in the group of provinces which lie between Beijing and Shanghai. For the previous fifty years, there had been no main centre of global smelting. The world's steel mills and aluminium and copper smelters had been spread fairly evenly across North America and western Europe, western Russia and Ukraine and Japan. There had been sharp shifts in the mix every now and then, most notably during the second Oil Crisis when Japan shut down its aluminium smelters and then again during the years after the collapse of the Soviet Union, when many of the Russian steel mills and other heavy industrial plants were closed. Still, the world's smelting capacity remained widely spread across many countries.

By 2014 things were different. After ten years of the mining boom, just six Chinese provinces – Hebei, Shandong, Shanxi, Jiangsu, Anhui and Henan – were home to nearly as much steel-making and aluminium smelting capacity as could be found in all of the rest of the world. They were also home to a large slice of the world's copper smelting base. And that was only in one region of China. As a country, China held a position of dominance in global smelting that had not been seen since the early years of the 1950s when the United States was the unchallenged leader.

That dominance had allowed China to reshape the mining and smelting industries. For one thing, it was no longer an accepted fact that that it took years of planning and construction to bring a smelter on-stream. China's engineers had dispelled that notion forever. During the mining boom, world-class aluminium smelters had been built from the ground up in 12 months. A good size steel mill had taken a bit longer.

More importantly than that, the Chinese dominance had led to the sweeping away of long-held notions of what was acceptable ore quality. The case of iron ore illustrates what happened. During the 1980s and 90s the Japanese steel mills had made the rules when it came to ore and coking coal quality. Phosphorous could not exceed a certain low limit, alumina and silica had to be within tight constraints, and so on. There were technical justifications for this. For one thing, land was very valuable along the shores of Tokyo Bay, so there was very limited space to conduct blending. If a mining company wanted to open a new mine, or sometimes even just develop a new pit, they had to go with mine plan in hand to the Japanese, seeking their approval. The Japanese executives would point out this or that flaw in the quality offering, and back the miners would go to re-think their plan, and add blending stages.

Technical justifications there may have been, but the Japanese also wielded quality as a negotiating stick. That changed when the Chinese burst onto the international stage. In the rush to secure feed for their blast furnaces, the Chinese steel mills had not spent too much time worrying about these finer points of ore quality. If a certain aspect of a particular ore created a problem, it might attract a lower price, but it still would find a buyer. The Fortescue Metals Group built its business on shipping ore to China that, ten years before, the Japanese steel mills would hardly even have considered.

The stainless steel sector provides another example. Indonesia had long been known as a nickel country but its deposits were difficult to treat. They were low grade laterites, and it was practically impossible to extract high quality nickel from them. They had one big advantage however: they were easy to mine. In other words, they were a cheap source of nickel in search of an application. That application was found when the realization dawned, that for many uses, stainless steel did not need high purity nickel. So it was that Indonesian "pig nickel",[46] laden with rubbish and anathema to western producers, was supplying a big part of the global market for stainless steel by end of the mining boom. Such was the power which could now be wielded by the Chinese via their dominance of the smelting sector.

If the mining boom had lifted the Chinese into a position of dominance in the world of smelting, it had done the same for it in the world of mining. China was, in 2014, by far the most important mining country on earth. It was easily the biggest miner of coal, bauxite, lead, zinc, tin, tungsten, rare earths and limestone, and among the top three in nearly everything else. The country had been the leader in global mining since the early 1990s, but during the mining boom it greatly extended this lead.

Even with this big increase in domestic mining, China had been forced to source much of its supply from overseas, only to find that most ore fields could not supply it. That was another remarkable aspect of the mining boom: the very high mineral prices of the period had only a limited impact on the development of new mining capacity outside of China.

Indeed, in each of the sectors of copper, iron ore, bauxite, coking coal and thermal coal there was really only one production region outside China which did most of the work in supplying what China could not supply for itself. In iron ore it was the Pilbara, in copper it was the Copperbelt, in bauxite it was the fields in West Kalimantan, in coking coal it was the east coast of Australia, and in thermal coal it was the mines of East and South Kalimantan. In nearly every other mining region of the world, the production increases seen over the ten years of the mining boom were no greater than during the ten years prior to the mining boom. In some regions, the rate of expansion was actually slower during the mining boom than before it. The sky-high prices did little to push mine development beyond the pace at which it would been developed anyway. Put differently, the mining boom exposed the fact that it was a very difficult task to increase production from most of the world's established fields.

To understand why this was, it is helpful to look first at the factors which allowed rapid expansion in those regions which did respond. In the bauxite and coal fields of Indonesia, production could be developed very quickly because the fields were made up of rich surface deposits, readily accessible, requiring very low capital expenditure and subject to almost no regulatory oversight.

In the Copperbelt, the mines could be rapidly brought on-stream because the deposits were known about and the basic infrastructure was already there. It was neglect and civil conflict which had led to their decline. Once the neglect and conflict were replaced by order and determined management, the fields rapidly came back to life.

The Pilbara was the only one of all the world's established mining regions where, during the mining boom, infrastructure-intensive mining developments were carried out with the scale and speed necessary to meet China's demands. The companies responsible for it – Rio Tinto, BHP Billiton and, latterly, Fortescue Metals – had the advantages of a series of known, large and easily accessible orebodies ready for development, expansion options for rail and port infrastructure and a supportive State government. To that could be added a capable set of management teams with plenty of access to capital. It was then a matter of skill and determination to get the job done.

So why did production from everywhere else struggle to respond? It was usually some mixture of three factors: a lack of suitable orebodies, a transport bottleneck with no ready expansion options and a difficult regulatory approval regime. The mining boom revealed that the majority of the world's mineral producing regions were seriously constrained in one way or another. Minerals hungry China could not wait for these regions to sort through their issues. Its domestic miners took matters into their own hands, ramping production up to unsustainable levels and seeking out neglected foreign production bases where the mineral output could be quickly increased. It worked well enough for ten years, but by 2014 the cracks were showing.

Six Years On

In the six years since 2014, there has been continuity in most of the trends which were developing towards the end of the boom.

China's appetite for metals and energy is still strong. As this demand has continued to grow, so too has China's smelting capacity. Over the last five years, most of the world's new smelters, be they in steel, aluminium, copper or any other metal, have been built in China. The construction of these plants has become what could be described as a well-oiled machine. Cheap money, government support, experienced engineers and (almost) assured off-take means that new capacity is easy for a company boardroom to approve. The new plants are built with up-to-date technology and, when this is coupled with the Chinese ability to construct and operate more efficiently than anywhere else, the result is that Chinese smelters typically have the lowest production costs in the world.

There is some domestic push-back against this continuing expansion.[47] This is happening in particular in the provinces with the heaviest concentration of smelting capacity, where air pollution has risen to seriously unhealthy levels. Hebei is probably the worst offender in this regard, and in that province there is a move to close the worst-polluting steel mills and coal-fired power stations. Not too much should be read into that. This sort of culling program has happened repeatedly over the course of the last few decades of Chinese industrialisation. It amounts to the trimming of sub-economic or poorly-performing capacity, making way for larger and better-designed plants built in more suitable locations.

China's mining production base has been unable to keep pace with the growth of the smelter capacity. Across the board, the country's mines were pushed too hard during the mining boom, and capacity was added by opening too many expensive-to-run mines. The result was that, while the mine production base was able to keep pace with industry's demands, it came at a high cost, both because the mines themselves were more difficult to operate and because the ore produced was poorer quality. The most obvious example was the iron ore sector but the same sort of thing had been done in nearly every other sector.

It comes as no surprise, therefore, that since 2014 the China's overall domestic mine production has been flat or in decline. In the coal sector, output is down by about 10%, having increased at a blistering pace between 2004 and 2014. In copper, the same thing can be said, only more so. The domestic mines are at the point of exhaustion and are being kept running at or near 2014 levels only because of the high price of copper and the absence of alternative supplies. As for iron ore, it has long since ceased to provide a substantial portion of the feed for the country's steel mills. It is now no more than a top-up supplier to the still-expanding Chinese steel-making sector. The bauxite operations, particularly those in the southern provinces of Guangxi and Guizhou, have continued to ramp-up but this has only been because of the lack of alternative supplies.

China's increasing smelter production coupled with this weakening mine production base means that it is leaning more heavily on the rest of the world for much of its iron, bauxite and copper ores. So the mining world outside of China is still under considerable pressure.

There has been a mixed response to this. The Pilbara has responded with big increases in mine production and steady expansion of its transport infrastructure. It is like it is a bottomless pit of ore and port expansion options. The ever-healthy iron ore price is a big factor driving this.

In copper, the established fields are still finding it hard to respond to the demand. One long lead-time project – Las Bambas – has come on-stream in Peru. It is a fairly rare event these days. Such projects are now very expensive to build and their continually declining head grades make them difficult investments to justify. No net production has been added in Chile, not much has been added in the Copperbelt and the United States and Australian annual outputs have fallen. Global copper production has grown however, thanks to the full recovery at Grasberg,[48] and a host of minor capacity expansions in a dozen countries.

In bauxite, the same general story can be told. The established fields have found it hard to mobilise new capacity. The two opportunistic fields – Kalimantan and coastal Malaysia – have been closed down by their governments. Virtually all of the incremental production in the last five years has come from the commissioning of multiple world-class projects in the West African nation of Guinea, most of which had been in prospect for a long time.

So as the 2020s dawn, the global mine production platforms which had been sufficient for the 1990s world are struggling to find their shape in the post-boom world. Can the Pilbara continue to be relied upon to supply the world's new demand for iron ore? Where is the copper to come from? Is the bauxite production platform stable?

Prices have fallen somewhat, although they remain well above pre-boom levels. They are also volatile, threatening to go up at any time. The supply and demand balance remains as tight as it has been during since 2004.

One reason for the slightly lower prices is that the mining companies have in the last five years made great strides in reducing their costs. During the mining boom, mine production costs escalated along with mineral prices: in other words, they went through the roof. There were several drivers of it. Firstly, and most important, was the fact that shortages developed almost immediately all along the supply chain. New equipment and spares were very hard to obtain. Truck tyres were in critically short supply for ten years,[49] earthmoving equipment was in the same position, as were explosives, some of the necessary chemicals, and even such items as brake pads and hardened steel digging blades. The cost of conducting engineering studies also sky-rocketed as the engineering design companies, having lived hand to mouth for decades, now had to pay big money to attract new staff.

Adding to the cost blow-out was the fact that management took its eye off the cost control ball. Before the boom, it would have been fair to say that vigilant cost management and careful project evaluation were the core requirements which a board of directors demanded of any senior mining executive. In the boom years, those skills took a back seat. What was needed instead was the ability to increase production, and drive up prices, through whatever means possible. It was all about seizing the revenues on offer in this bonanza. No-one got any plaudits or promotions for keeping costs down.

This drive to get more production extended to acquiring other companies and this, in turn, led to a few of the more memorable episodes of the mining boom. One of the most memorable was Rio Tinto's friendly – some would say too friendly – take-over of the aluminium producer, Alcan. That episode began when Glencore, a newcomer to the ranks of mining majors, brokered a three-way merger of its own aluminium assets and those of the two Russian producers, SUAL and Rusal. The new company, United Company Rusal, was formed in March 2006[50] and became the world's biggest producer of aluminium, and also one of the larger companies in the bauxite and alumina sectors.

Suddenly, for some reason, the title of "world's largest aluminium producer" became a coveted one. In hot pursuit of that title, in early 2007, Alcoa, which had fallen to second place after the Rusal merger, announced a bid for Alcan, third placed in the aluminium production rankings. That started an intense round of aluminium companies sizing each other up. BHP Billiton was reportedly preparing a bid for Alcoa, and CVRD was looking at Alcan. It is at this point that the Rio Tinto executive team enters the pages of history. In June 2007, they finalised a takeover offer for Alcan which blew everyone else away. The bid was 33% higher than Alcoa's.[16] Why they made such a generous offer is unclear to this day. The bauxite price was flat and showing no sign of rising, alumina was in oversupply, and aluminium smelters were being built all over the place in China. Why pay an unwarranted premium to get into a business like that? It wouldn't even get them the title of world's largest aluminium producer. Unsurprisingly, the Rio bid was unanimously accepted by Alcan's board of directors.

Rio Tinto was not alone in using mergers and acquisitions to build production in the early years of the mining boom. Other big companies also tried their luck. Their main targets were the long established North American and Australian mid-tier base metals companies. BHP Billiton launched a successful bid for Western Mining in 2005, and in that same year Noranda and Falconbridge merged. This merged entity was acquired by Xstrata in 2006. Xstrata had already made a name for itself by buying Mount Isa Mines in 2002. Also in 2006, Vale (formerly CVRD) acquired Inco, and Phelps Dodge was acquired by Freeport McMoran. Asarco was already gone, having become part of Grupo Mexico in 1999. The only mid-tier North American base metals companies left standing at the end of 2006 were Alcan and Teck Cominco. Alcan was gone the next year. Which left just Teck Cominco. It became Teck Resources in 2008.

The last big M+A event of the mining boom was the biggest of them all. In early 2008, BHP Billiton launched a takeover bid for Rio Tinto, where the executive team was distracted trying to figure out what to do with its Alcan albatross. The bid was driven by the cost savings and production increases which could be made by combining the Pilbara operations of the two companies. Being the two biggest mining companies in the world, if the takeover had been successful it would have created a mining company of an unprecedented size and market power. But it was not to be. Resistance from the regulatory authorities slowed things down, and the Global Financial Crisis killed it off.

In the years since the height of the boom, cost control has made a comeback. It is remarkable how quickly and substantially unit production costs could be reduced without impacting production. BHP Billiton cut their unit costs nearly in half, in both iron ore and coal, between 2012 and 2016. Rio Tinto did something similar.[51] In 2020 the global mining production base was a much leaner machine than it was in 2014.

There is plenty more of that to come. This is because, during next thirty years, global mining will bring with it a persistent oversupply of a kind rarely seen in global markets. That issue is explored in the fourth book of this series, *Oversupply: Global Mining to 2050.*

References

1 *China Steel: China's emerging steel industry,* Stephen Labson, Peter Gooday and Andrew Manson, ABARE Research Report 95.4, Australian Bureau of Agriculture and Resource Economics, 1995

2 *An analysis of China's grain production: looking backward and forward,* Weifeng Zhang et al, Food and Energy Security, 2014

3 *The Mineral Industry of China,* Minerals Yearbook Area Reports 1980, US Bureau of Mines

4 *How China Built a Steel Behemoth and Convulsed World Trade,* Chuin-Wei Yap, Wall Street Journal, 24 December 2018

5 *China's Economy: A Basic Guide,* Christopher Howe, Granada Publishing, 1980

6 *Iron and Steel,* Anthony Peters, Mineral Yearbook 1990, US Bureau of Mines

7 *The Mineral Industry of China,* Minerals Yearbook Area Reports 1990, US Bureau of Mines

8 *Construction industry in China's regional economy: 1990 to 1998,* Sun Sheng Han and George Ofori, Construction Management and Economics, No 19, 2001

9 *China's Iron and Steel Industry,* Mission to China, Australian Department of Trade, Australian Govt Publishing Services 1985

10 *Historical statistics for mineral and material commodities in the United States,* Thomas Kelly and Grecia Matos, United States Geological Survey, 2014

11 *Steel Statistical Yearbook,* World Steel Institute, 2003

12 *Vale – Our History,* Vale Corporate Publications, 2012

13 *Copper,* Daniel L Edelstein, United States Geological Survey, 2000

14 *Governing the Extractive Sector: the Politics of Globalisation and Copper Policy in Chile,* Jewellord T Nem Singh, Journal of Critical Globalisation Studies, Vol 3, 2010

15 *Chile's Return to Democracy,* Pamela Constable and Arturo Valenzuela, Foreign Affairs, Winter 1989/90

16 *The Australian Exploration Boom 1965-72-'73,* PJ Roberts, Bureau of Mineral Resources, Geology and Geophysics, 1974

17 *Rio Tinto grabs Alcan in mining's largest-ever deal,* Michelle Weise Brockman, Mining Journal, July 13 2007

18 *The Great Housing Boom of China,* Kaiji Chen and Yi Wen, CQER Working Paper 15-03, Federal Reserve Bank of Atlanta, 2015

19 *Steel Statistical Yearbook 2004,* International Iron and Steel Institute, 2004

20 *The recent rise in commodity prices: a long-run perspective,* John O'Connor and David Orsmond, Reserve Bank of Australia Bulletin, April 2007

21 *Rio Tinto plans capital return as profits soar,* Mining Journal, 3 February 2006

22 *One year of my blood: the exploitation of migrant construction workers in Beijing,* Human Rights Watch, March 2008

23 *A new era for manufacturing in China,* Karen Eloot, Alan Huang, Martin Lehnich, McKinsey Quarterly, June 2013

24 *Industrialisation in China,* Loren Brandt, Debin Ma and Thomas Rawski, Institute of Labour Economics, Discussion Paper no. 10096, July 2016

25 *China's toxic soil,* The Economist, 8 June 2017

26 *Substitution trend in the copper market,* B Grimm and Li Lan, paper presented at 7th Asian Copper Conference, Metal Bulletin, 15-16 September 2011

27 *Production history of the Bingham Mining District,* Ken Krahulec, Utah Geological Survey, September 2018

28 *Productivity in the Chilean copper mining industry,* National Productivity Commission of Chile, 2017

29 *At the crossroads: mining and political change on the Katangese-Zambian Copperbelt,* Miles Larmer, Oxford Handbooks On-line, 2016

30 *An overview of copper mining in Zambia's Copperbelt province,* Pardon Sinkala et al, Proceedings of the Spring Meeting of the MMIJ, Hokkaido University, June 2018

31 *Regulating Foreign Direct Investments in resource-dependent African countries: the case of Chinese investments in Zambia's copper mining sector,* Beyongo Mukete Dynamic, thesis submitted for PhD, Australian National University, 2018

32 *Comalco's development of Queensland bauxite, 1955-1975,* David Lee, Wiley On-line Library, 2016

33 *Guinea: selected issues and statistical appendix,* IMF Country Report No 08/20, January 2008

34 *Mining and Development in Indonesia: An Overview of the Regulatory Framework and Policies,* Bernadette Devi and Dody Prayogo, Sustainable Mining Institute, 2013

35 *Resource Nationalism in Indonesia – effects of the 2014 mineral export ban,* United States Geological Survey, September 2016

36 *Tracks from the past, transport for the future: China's railway industry 1990 to 2008,* World Bank, 2009

37 *Coal in India 2015,* Kate Penny and Ian Cronshaw, Office of the Chief Economist, Department of Industry and Science, Australian Government, June 2015

38 *Indian coal power plants kill 120,000 people each year, says Greenpeace,* The Guardian, 11 March 2013

39 *A hunger for coal threatens the heart of Borneo,* The Borneo Project, May 2014

40 Black coal in Australia, MB Huleatt, Bureau of Mineral Resources, Australian Mineral Industry Quarterly, 34, 1981

41 *Freightline 4: Australian coal freight transport,* Department of Infrastructure and Regional Development, Australian Government, September 2016

42 *Iron Country: Unlocking the Pilbara,* David Lee, Minerals Council of Australia, June 2015

43 *Transportation of iron ore: a case study of the northern Brazilian region,* Maricruz Cepeda and Rafaelo Kneipp, conference paper, Proceedings of 11th International Seminar on Inland Waterways and waterborne Transportation, October 2019

44 *Karnataka export ban led to pile-up of 12 million tonnes of iron ore,* Hellenic Shipping News, March 2020

45 *Infrastructure Investment in China,* Kelsey Wilkins and Andrew Zurawski, RBA Bulletin, June 2014

46 *Industry experts deem nickel pig iron innovations the pressing issue for 2014,* Informa Insights, November 2013

47 *China's Hebei Province Fights for Blue Skies,* World Bank News, World Bank, 5 June 2019

48 *Picking up the pieces: Indonesian mine collapse,* Malevikar Santhebennur, Australian Mining, 19 July 2013

49 *Tyre shortage slowing miner's expansion,* Mining Monthly, 13 July 2005

50 United Company Rusal formation, Rusal website

51 *Rio Tinto unveils cost-saving measures,* Mining Journal, January 23 2009

Made in the USA
Monee, IL
04 November 2026

67380389R00046